THE
POTATO EATER

The raw true story of Padric, a gay
hustler from the Bronx who spent
1941-1965 in and out of 20 prisons

ALISON LESLIE GOLD

TMI Publishing, Providence, RI
www.tmipublishing.com

Author's website: www.AlisonLeslieGold.com
https://facebook.com/Alison Leslie Gold

The Potato Eater

TMI Publishing
61 Doyle Avenue
Providence, RI 02906
www.tmipublishing.com

Cover by Hanaan Rosenthal

ISBN: 978-1-938371-19-6

Also by Alison Leslie Gold

Nonfiction

Anne Frank Remembered: The Story of the Woman who Helped to Hide the Frank Family (with Miep Gies)

Memories of Anne Frank: Reflections of a Childhood Friend

Fiet's Vase and Other Stories of Survival, Europe 1939-1945

A Special Fate: Chiune Sugihara: Hero of the Holocaust

Lost and Found

Love in the Second Act

Fiction

Clairvoyant

The Devil's Mistress

The Woman Who Brought Matisse Back from the Dead

Elephant in the Living Room (with Darin Elliott)

*Look for **Alison Leslie Gold** on Facebook*

*Or visit: **www.AlisonLeslieGold.com***

potato /n. & v. (Sp. patata var. of BATATO) PL. **-oes.**
Phrases: **hot potato** *colloq.* a controversial or awkward
matter or situation. *meat and potatoes;* see MEAT n. **small
potatoes** *colloq.* (a person who or thing which is) insig-
nificant or unimportant. **the (clean) potato** *colloq.* the
correct or socially acceptable thing; a socially acceptable
or honorable person.

AUTHOR'S NOTE

When I first met Padric McGarry in 1976 he looked like the edgy singer-songbird Gwen Stefani, or like a tall, henna-haired Veronica Lake from time past Hollywood. He would fling his shoulder length hair when he turned his head, was tall, poised, had alert, hazel eyes that didn't miss a thing. In a New York ("Noo" York, Get "outta" here) accent, he described himself as "flaming, not nelly, with a skinny, fruit body." We met in New York when he was fifty-one years old. When I last saw him in 1982, he was vastly altered, only sputtering bits of charcoal remained of that flame. Shortly afterwards I received a letter from a bereft friend describing a massive heart attack in San Diego that doused the fire entirely.

Padric asked me to write his biography after I interviewed him for an article I was hired to do for a magazine. I was intrigued and did further interviews with him. Additionally, he gave me other material he'd been gathering that related to his life. Time stole me away; other writings were undertaken pushing him to the back of my mind.

Ten books were published as I crisscrossed the country and world; matured, sank and bobbed back.

Recently, coming up for air, thoughts of Padric returned. I began a search through disordered archives for our papers and tapes and I found them buried inside a cardboard carton that had been stored for almost thirty years. The rubber bands had stiffened; they disintegrated and stuck to batched pages and antiquated plastic cassette cases when I began to peel them away.

Now assembled, this narrative offers up a platter of raw crudités that have been dipped into a vinaigrette mixed from those pungent materials assembled long ago. These include taped interviews, biographical material from an unfinished fictionalized memoir that Padric and his friend Spencer had partially crafted that he urged me, if useful, to draw from, fragments of remembered conversation and events, my article in *Blueboy Magazine*, our fact-based story published in *Christopher Street*, a few letters and my own imagination. Not surprisingly, Padric had his set-pieces and, with small variation, they were told and re-told, to me, to Spencer, in talks he gave, over French toast and coffee in a hundred coffee shops in New York. Those who knew him still remember his storytelling.

Wherever possible, I use Padric's own words—raw, profane, overflowing with expletives—to evoke his culture along with those quintessential gay times, now dated and long past. In my mind, Padric's vernacular forged him into the brassy alloy he became and nowhere more so than in repeated colorful stories in which some of the sexual images are quite explicit. Prudes beware.

While cherry picking from his factual history, I've changed some names and identifying details to protect privacy of individuals. The elements of Padric's story have been expanded, textured, occasionally fictionalized and molded into a sculpture made of a hard bell-metal in the shape of a tall, slim man of Irish-American descent who was born out of wedlock in 1925 in the Bronx and didn't want his experience as a gay man in a straight world to be forgotten. This book also memorializes the pre-AIDS halcyon summers on Fire Island, where being gay became a badge and not a blight.

Grateful thanks to Spencer Beach for shared material, Gail Vanderhoof and Helle Valborg Goldman for editorial help and to TMI Press for shepherding Padric's story into this vastly altered century.

Alison Leslie Gold
New York, 2015

FROM AN AUDIO TAPE MADE
IN 1977 IN NEW YORK CITY

I was 16 when I was arrested for corrupting the morals of soldiers and sailors, blocking a public doorway, and disturbing the peace. In prison I began to grow up and learn. I learned how to pick pockets, how to open five kinds of safes, how to forge checks, how to work second story, how to boost. We'd practice there. I learned all the necessary things to spend 20 more years in different prisons. Rikers Island was my junior high school. Sing Sing and Dannemora State were my high schools. The chain gang and Leavenworth were my colleges.

Immediately I had 'Homosexual, Degenerate, Cock Sucker' stamped on my records so I was rarely in population with the rest of the men. I was kept in segregation with junkie queens, wino queens, booster queens, prick peddlers, drag queens and some men who just preferred to be in the homo block where they were adored and given sexual comfort. Life in segregation with those mad sissies was like being caged with a mass of mad, screaming peacocks.

Sex was always instant and quick—you were ever-ready. I knew that the best way to a man's heart in prison was through his prick or asshole, and learned quickly to have at least five husbands. It was smart to have a man in the kitchen because the food was so terrible— connections for sandwiches. A man in the laundry so I could look pretty. A man in the library so I could keep my culture and intellect high. A man in the hospital for little goodies like cold cream. Vaseline. Shampoo. A man working in one of the factories because he earned money—to have a Daddy with money.

I became a seminal dump. My only reality was the second of ejaculation. I'd choose the freakiest of mates—Neanderthals— humpy-punky but masculine. I was sometimes known as Millicent Duchess of Southerland, sometimes as Tarzana because I could swing up through the catwalks from tier to tier. If I had a boyfriend, we'd make arrangements between count time when the guards came by, I'd swing up to his tier, turn the trick, and swing back down in a matter of minutes.

I fell madly in love with a big Irish donkey who worked in the kitchen and was almost directly above me on the second tier. We began our romance. He'd write me love notes. He'd get a big hard-on and bang it on the locker to let me know, like the cave man beating his chest. We'd send each other our jockey shorts, and occasionally we'd exchange tiny bottles of seminal fluid. I'd sing to him because we almost never got together.

Another I remember vividly, a red neck from Alabama, had an 11 inch prick. There was a bouquet of flowers, a battleship and three little pigs tattooed on the head. I loved to trick with him, get it hard just to look at the gallery of tattoos. My longest encounter? Well, in federal prison, the elite country club, I could put up a blanket in front of my cell and we could get buck naked and go to bed, and have, gee, a half hour. That's like 10 hours out here.

Often, if men don't come in gay, time erodes their heterosexual resistance to what they've been trained to believe is abnormality. The love hunger begins, they get tired of beating their meat. Without sex and love the soul shrivels. Their will to live says, 'Alright, if I've got to suck a prick or get fucked to feel some peace, okay okay.' Many can't ever get over the experience of prison sexuality when they get out. In my case, after I got out for good, I was unpassionate for the longest time because of the deadly habit in prison of sex under tension.

❖

A FAMILY. Twelve children and two adults—marital status unknown—crossed the Atlantic from Ireland. The adults couldn't cope so they swaddled the children with every piece of clothing they could grab from a church rummage and took the ferry from South Ferry, Manhattan to St. George, Staten Island, in search of orphanages run by the Catholic Church. Clamping the small ones on their laps, lining up the larger ones, the family crowded onto wooden benches on the deck of the drab, double-ended boat with their backs to lower Manhattan's skyscrapers. The Statue of Liberty was shadowed in murk because of a leaden sky; close by, freighters were anchored at sea waiting for available docks in order to unload cargoes.

Street venders on Staten Island hawked pills that would protect against approaching Halley's Comet. Newspaper boys shouted to alert those disembarking the ferry to wear helmets or head-covers against the dangerous showers of debris that were about to fall on their heads should the comet pass too close.

The parents picked up a copy of *The Daily News*, read, circled in red crayon:

…it is believed that the comet's tail is full of deadly cyanogen gas. Planet Earth may hurtle straight into this brew like a cannonball. It's likely that the skies will curdle and the seas will boil and every living soul will smother. It's calculated that the world will end sometime between 10:20 P.M. and midnight on Wednesday, the 18th of May 1910.

Were we fools to leave Ireland, the mother wondered.

A priest separated the girl and boy children. The girls went into the Loretta Convent, the boys were sent to St. Joseph's Seminary. No more information about the parents exists, except a rumor that they both either died or disappeared, or, perhaps, that the wife died of a broken heart. These variations of factless rumors were told to him by Mary, his mother, at different times.

There was something funny—peculiar not haha—about the stories. Maybe Mary made them up? Padric never saw one souvenir or trace of her parents. Nor was there a family rosary left behind. Nothing.

Several little girls in the Loretta Orphanage got headaches that caused a high fever. Soon these wee girls were unable to move their limbs. The doctor visited, called the illness poliomyelitis. The Sisters referred to it as infantile paralysis. The older children renamed it "The Crippler."

The nuns blamed it on the poor, dirty Italian immigrants who had begun to move onto Staten Island.

God forgive them!

Afraid that animals were the carriers, the City of New York exterminated seventy thousand cats. Mother Superior told Sister Bright to hang a giant flytrap in the kitchen at the orphanage. Also, a bold red warning sign was nailed onto the front door by the city officials.

Mary had every symptom but didn't get polio.

Sister Aida caught Mary drinking vinegar and kicked her out of the convent school. This was 1923, Mary was thirteen.

Mary would never tell what she did or where she went once she went out into the world.

Padric and another child—twins—were born on April 10, 1925 when Mary was fifteen years old. She gave birth at the House of The Good Shepherd, a Catholic hospital for unwed mothers. Good Friday happened to fall on April 10th in 1925. The home for unwed mothers was close by Battery Park, in view of the clock tower at the edge of the pier that sounded the signals for watches kept on board ships. His twin—brother? sister?—Mary didn't remember which—either strangled on the umbilical cord or was stillborn.

When Padric began teething, Mary scrounged a piece of bacon rind to chew. She attached string to the rind and tied it to his wrist.

The Bronx neighborhood was made up of Irish, Scottish, Eastern Europeans and Jews. Mary lived with a common-law husband—Mickey McGarry—who read the *Bronx Home News*. Sometimes he read the *Journal American*. For laughs they called Padric "Skippy" like the cartoon in the *Journal American*.

Mary loudly cursed rich people and priests. She was a tall woman, five feet eight-and-a-half with light, almost kinky, auburn hair, that she bobbed when Padric was very small and let frizzle later on. She was proud of its burnished gloss that showed various red highlights in sunlight, tried to keep it up as best she could with dye after it started going gray. She had broad, child-bearing hips, was small-boned and slender, never fat, and had a mean little mouth. She had a crooked nose from her fall down some steps, nice hazel eyes, terrible eyebrows that Padric plucked for her once in a while. Mary never wore perfume or did her nails. Her idea of makeup was Lady Esther Outdoor Girl Powder along with a couple of rouge spots on the cheeks. She claimed that she took Padric to Rudolph Valentino's funeral at Saint Malachy's Church on West Forty-Ninth Street in Manhattan when he was one. Padric had no way to prove it, but never believed her. She just wasn't the type to want to see a dead man even if he was a big cheese.

He was confirmed at Saint Luke's Church by Cardinal Spellman. Although Mickey and Mary weren't married, they used Mickey's last name—McGarry—and because Padric had a round bottom, kids taunted him in singsong:

Here comes Padric McGarry's ass,

His head is following later.

He slept on a narrow, saggy bed in a small room.

Mickey woke him in the middle of the night. A tin bucket was hanging from his big fist.

Don't forget, Skippy, tell them to take the head off.

Mickey called it, 'rushing the growler.' Padric had to put on a coat and take the bucket to the Beer Garden on the next block where the bartender filled the bucket for twenty-five cents.

Take the head off it, Padric demanded, like Mickey had told him to say, to get more beer, less foam, so he could take a lick of foam too.

When he got whooping cough, Mickey made a paste of garlic and lard. Mary massaged it into his back. Afterwards, she handed him Katzenjammer Kids cartoons in the papers to look at. But Padric didn't like the Katzenjammer Kids, they were too stupid. He stacked the newspapers on a chair, slept beneath a cloud of garlic.

He spent his childhood in the South Bronx, a neighborhood known as the "138th Street Neighborhood" that stretched between Cypress Avenue and Third Avenue. His first memory: A sunless apartment on 135th Street, a brown-brick apartment building with a chipped stoop. Their apartment had five small rooms furnished with dark Grand Rapids furniture, and a Philco radio.

The boys in the neighborhood played frantic handball against the building, slapping the ball so hard it sang in his ears. Mary got hit in the breast by a hard, black handball. It deflated her full breasts. The only time they swelled up from then on was when she gave birth. That's also the only time she ever drank beer.

Aunt Rose entered the Joseph P. Day Cup at Manhattan Beach. The story came down to Padric that Aunt Rose swam three-and-a-half miles in the same race with the record-holding Helen Wainwright and when Aunt Rose emerged from the water, she was in third place and drank an entire bottle of Jameson whiskey to warm herself back up.

Aunt Betty took Padric to mass on Good Friday.

The Priest sermonized: But death did not vanquish him. The gospel explains that on the Sunday morning after the Friday of the Crucifixion the tomb was found empty and that Jesus rose again from the dead. He appeared to Peter, to James, to all the apostles including Thomas-the-Doubter and then to more than five hundred brethren. You see, Easter followed the Crucifixion and turned Black Friday into Good Friday because Jesus had risen. I am the resurrection and the life; he that believeth in me, though he were dead, yet shall he live. And whosoever liveth and believeth in me shall never die. Open to John 11:25:26.

Padric felt dizzy.

I was born on Good Friday, he whispered to Aunt Betty.

He fainted when he stood up.

A stout man carried him outside the church into too bright sunshine. Padric came to, was being tickled by the black hairs on the man's wrists sticking out of the blue Sunday suit. Aunt Betty had him sit down on the curb with his head between his knees.

Does crucifixion hurt, Aunt Betty?

To be nailed to a cross? You bet it does Patty. It's a slow agony. Poor sod.

Padric felt hot and cold chills.

That's why you must eat everything on your plate Patty. Get strong and stay strong. Now get up.

Padric put eyebrow pencil on Mary's eyebrows. He took her to Radio City Music Hall to see *Gone With the Wind* feeling like a prince in the majestic foyer fifty feet high. And wishing Mary would walk slower as she pulled him past William Zorach's sculpted *Dancing Figure* in the main lounge, past Gwen Lux's *Eve* in the main foyer. They tramped up the grand stairway to the first mezzanine and he gaped at Robert Laurent's *Goose Girl* and even dared to touch the henna-colored Brocatelle wall covering with the soft tips of his princely hand. He glimpsed himself in the floor-to-ceiling gold-leaf mirrors, saw that the prince did have a fat ass and Mary had wide hips. While they waited in their cushy seats for the show to begin, lights telescoped and suffused the curved interior with glowing pastel colors. Where were the lights coming from, he wondered.

For the rest of his life Padric could remember almost every line in *Gone With the Wind*.

Padric stood on a kitchen chair that was pushed against the kitchen table. Mary showed him how to mash already peeled, dirty white potatoes real good in a big bowl she'd gotten for free at the movies.

Add salt.

He cautiously sprinkled in a pinch of salt.

More.

He tossed in a large spoon, filled to the brim.

Add flour.

He did.

More.

He powdered more flour over the mix, looked up for her next instruction. None were given.

She dripped hot melted, strong-smelling bacon fat into the mashed potatoes, then laid out a towel over which she tossed more flour. She showed Padric how to use a rolling pin and roll the big gop of potatoes out then how to cut rounds. She cooked the rounds in a greasy pan side by side. Mary turned them, pricked them with a fork, lay them in two piles on a plate.

She trimmed the rind off a bacon rasher and cooked it in the same pan until black smoke rose and the room smelled like burnt fat—a very nice smell. She lowered the fire, added a knob of butter to the pan, then quickly removed the bacon, and began breaking egg after egg into the hot butter and blackish bacon grease.

Don't let the eggs frizzle when you make this, she told him. Watch me.

The eggs got brown around the edges. Mary tipped the pan and some of the hot fat glazed the yolks with streaks of burnt black.

They sat down and ate bacon, eggs and potato cakes at the kitchen table. That day for no reason that he knew of, he was allowed to eat all he wanted. It was the most delicious and most filling meal he'd ever tasted before or after. Probably the only time he felt entirely satiated. Mary let him taste her bitter, hot coffee. She drank it strong and black. Always had. Always would.

Mary took him to the German Swedish Hall up on the hill between Willis Avenue and Alexander for a Christmas pageant.

I have someone to see. Be good, she whispered, giving his arm a sharp pinch and pressing him into a straight-backed chair in the front row. She walked away. When the pageant was over, he got into the line with the rest of the kids to go up on stage and walk past Santa Claus and receive a present.

When Padric got up there, Santa asked, Where's your Mommy?

She had to go.

I can't give you a present without a parent.

Padric hung around until the last kid got his present, then he went up to Santa again.

Can I have my present now?

Santa shook his head.

Padric walked home by himself. He knew the neighborhood streets very well, waited for the light to change before he crossed at each corner as Mickey had taught him to do.

Mary was asleep.

Stupefied from a brew she had consumed, Mary stood on a chair and fell to the floor.

Another time, she threw herself down the front steps, broke her nose, which stayed crooked.

Mary carried fourteen children in her belly at different times. Four survived, the others either miscarried or were born dead. Padric believed that all four of the survivors were conceived by different fathers.

Winter. Padric was four. He walked with Mary over to 132 Street between St. Ann's and Cypress. They went up to visit Matt, the neighborhood butcher, who lived alone on the second floor of a house. They climbed the front stairway and Mary pressed a bell. Matt came to the door in a red watered silk bathrobe and blue pajamas and invited them inside where the radiators hissed steam.

They left Padric on a red stool in the tiny kitchen that was off to the side.

Mary called back to him, Stay there.

He wiggled off the stool in order to look around. He found a box under the sink that said Gold Dust Twins. Also a toilet plunger and a mousetrap. He stuck his hand inside the box and felt sticky powder. The feeling was like sucking a lemon. The powder stuck to his clammy hand.

He walked into the bedroom rubbing his hand on the front of his shirt. Mary was stretched cross-wise on the bed. Matt the Butcher was naked from the waist down, on top of her, pushing down. Matt was wearing an undershirt that was shoved up almost to his neck, exposing patches of curly brown hair on his strong back and neck. Padric watched Matt's ass move up and down, noticed pink splotches on his ass flesh. Matt turned and smiled, showing big white teeth, one gold on top under his thin, brown moustache.

Padric walked around the bottom of the bed and up toward the middle, on the side where Mary's head was. She didn't notice him. He smelled her shampoo. Matt kept pumping. Padric touched Mary's face, she asked, What do you want.

I'm hungry.

There's chocolate candy in my pocketbook.

Padric looked inside her purse and clasped the chocolate suckers at the linty bottom, then stood near the ash-filled coal stove and sucked two at once. He went back to the doorway to watch Matt pump. He decided he would tell Matt, Go fry an egg.

When Padric started school he was advanced half a year because he was ahead of his class in everything.

He asked his teacher, Why does the compass needle always point to the North?

A good question.

Is the shadowy moon that we see in the daytime for children, since they can't stay up late enough at night to see the other moon?

A very good question.

Why is there a silent E?

You talk too much.

During the Depression beggars went from building to building. They sang for a few pennies that people tossed at them. When Mary wasn't home, Padric stood in the back courtyard behind the building. He sang a song he'd heard Aunt Betty sing after a few drinks:

> *They brought her to the city,*
> *And she faded slowly there*
> *Consumption has no pity*
> *For blue eyes and golden hair.*

A few pennies jangled onto the courtyard. After that he sang from the tar paper covered roof or while standing on the slatted fire escape landing. Another of Aunt Betty's songs,

> *All her bright golden hair*
> *Tarnished with rust,*
> *She that was young and fair,*
> *Fallen to dust.*

He remembered grass and trees and bushes and a big blanket. He was lost. He found his way to the corner, crossed the street, talked to a retarded little girl holding the hand of a man who had big, rosy cheeks.

A policeman carried him up the steps at 135th Street. Mary and Mickey stood on the top step. Mickey must have cut himself shaving since a torn piece of toilet tissue was stuck to his chin. There was one bright spot of almost black dried blood. Mary was rude to the cop and Mickey ass-licked him.

Mary boiled hot water. She poured it into cups, added ketchup. She mixed the ketchup in with a spoon for tomato soup.

He got nosebleeds. When he had a bad bleed Mary laid a wet cloth across his forehead and nose. At the same time she put a hot water bottle wrapped with a dishtowel under his feet. When he got toothaches a clove was pressed between the tooth and gum. He took out the clove because it was bitter.

Don't make me yell at you. I'll need my breath when I'm dying, Padric.

He was seven or maybe younger. It was winter, probably 1933, a heavy snowstorm had fallen. It was his first chance to use a Christmas gift given by his two alcoholic aunts, Betty and Rose—a Silver King sled. Like everyone in the neighborhood who had one, Padric struggled to get to St. Mary's Park.

All afternoon he dragged the sled up slushy hills and sledded down. He wore a padded sky-blue snowsuit. It began to get dark and he knew he should go but stayed for a few more slides. A big Armenian kid, maybe twelve or thirteen, approached him at the bottom of the hill.

I'll carry your sled up if you let me ride down the hill with you.

Sure.

The Armenian kid carried up the sled and then laid on top of him as they slid down the hill. He was warm and not heavy at all.

Finally it was really dark except that the snow seemed lit by itself.

I have to go home otherwise my mother will kill me.

The Armenian kid carried the sled and they walked to Cypress Avenue together.

Reaching Padric's building, the kid led him behind the stairway, where children's carriages and other junk got stuffed. He put his sled down on the floor in a dark corner.

The kid told Padric, Sit on it.

Padric did. The kid unzipped his coat, took it off and put it under Padric's ass. Then he pulled down Padric's blue snowsuit, his pants, and his jockey shorts and pushed Padric down onto the sled, like they were going to go downhill again. The kid laid himself down on top of him. Something was pushed into his behind, the weight of the boy pushed him into the coat. Then the boy got up. Padric felt wet on his ass, down his crack, and at the base of his back. Melted snow was pooled under the sled. The boy took out a blue folded handkerchief and wiped away the wet, even in the crack then helped Padric put his clothes back on, layer by layer.

I'll take you home. It's suppertime.

After they'd climbed the steps the kid said, I'll meet you tomorrow. We can belly whop again. Meet me at the Cypress Avenue entrance to the park.

The next day Padric stood at Cypress Avenue in the cold with his sled. He waited until it got dark, but the kid didn't come.

The day after he waited again. Again he didn't show.

The snow began to melt. Padric stood with his sled— one last day—and waited but still the kid didn't come. Soon the snow was entirely gone and only lumps of dog shit and garbage that was underneath remained.

For months Padric asked everyone in the neighborhood if they knew a big Armenian kid, knew where he lived? Even though no one in the neighborhood seemed to know him, Padric kept looking out for him wherever he was.

Mary put a nickel into his hand.

Buy white ones. Look for the ones that are well shaped, that are firm. Be sure they're free of blemishes or sunburn. Watch out for sprouts or shrivels.

He walked to the Jewish market. He looked for white potatoes but all he saw were brown-skinned ones, also red ones. Some were round, some oval. He didn't know what to do.

Are they white?

They're russet Idahos.

He didn't know what to do.

Mama, my clothes are torn, I want some new clothes. Padric begged.

Mary took Padric into her arms.

I do the best I can. I wish you had good clothes, too.

Padric thought, She must love me a lot.

When Mary wasn't home Padric went to her closet and took down her "good" wool dress, lowered it over his head.

Mrs. Kreutzer was the lady upstairs. She read the *Daily Worker*. Her legs and fingers were gnarled-up from rheumatism. She was always complaining about the pain in her hands. Padric went up to see her often. She showed him an old-fashioned lady's ring, gold, with a big lavender amethyst, six or eight carats and two small, pale amethysts and a couple of diamond chips. She let him hold the ring and look at it over by the window, or by lamplight. Often he came up just to look at the ring.

Once when she was in the kitchen, he reached into the polished mosaic box that she kept on a spindly little table in her front room. The ring was there. He wanted to give it to Mary—to put on her second finger—so he shoved the ring into the pocket of his knickers and went downstairs to his own apartment on the fourth floor.

He wrapped the ring in tissue paper, tied it with a tartan plaid ribbon he found behind the front door. He tip-toed into the bedroom. Mary was stretched out in the bed. He gave her the ring.

When she opened it she didn't smile.

It's Mrs. Kreutzer's isn't it?

Padric was shocked that she didn't put it on her finger.

Take it right back upstairs and put it on Mrs. Kreutzer's table. If she sees you, tell her you took it by mistake.

His eyes filled with very hot tears. He went back upstairs and put it back in its mosaic box. Mrs. Kreutzer hadn't noticed that it was missing.

Aunt Rosie's boyfriend, who was called Uncle Johnny (though not a real uncle, since she was married to Joey Watson), always hung his jacket on the back of a chair. His pockets were full of change that could pay for double feature at the movie house along with candy and soda. Padric never missed dipping in for a few coins until Uncle Johnny got wise.

Padric was hungry all the time.

Padric was bitten by a dog. The dog's slobber wetted the break in the skin where the sharp teeth had broken through.

The school nurse warned him, You'll get delirious. Air will hurt your skin. You'll have a clonic convulsion during which you'll think that you're struggling with someone. Your pupils will dilate. You will spit saliva in little pools onto my linoleum. Between convulsions, you'll get dressed, stand at the window, look out, then strip again, have another convulsion. You've got to have rabies shots!

Padric had heard that rabies shots were painful needles in the tender skin of his stomach every day for twenty-one days.

No I won't. I don't care if I die.

Mary bundled him up and dragged him through a downpour to the clinic.

No!

The doctor spoke convincingly to Padric, not to Mary. After you're dead I'll make an incision with a scalpel across your head. I'll have access to your skull. I'll peel back the skin, and then with a sharp saw I'll split your skull bone in order to remove your brain. I'll discard your head for incineration, and take a small sample from your grey matter with a tweezers. That's when I'll know I was right, that you needed these shots but it will be too late.

Padric clamped his hand over the doctor's leathery mouth. The nurse prepared needles filled with infected rabbit spinal cord fluid that had been dried.

He got these terrible rabies shots in a Bronx clinic for 21 days.

After the last ones Mary bought him a string of maple syrup-flavored rock candy that he tried to let slowly melt in his mouth and not crunch between his teeth. He couldn't resist one crunch and heard a molar crack. He went back to school in time for Arbor Day. Mary put a Bumble Bee tuna sandwich and an apple into a paper bag.

Padric wore a blue suit, knickers, long black stockings, a big white collar and bow tie with a satin armband for his First Holy Communion.

Mickey got paid by the electric company on Fridays, earned thirty-five dollars a week. Every Friday night he gave Mary the week's pay envelope for food. One Friday she gave Padric the black oilcloth shopping bag, a ten-dollar bill, and a list. She blasted Padric with fishy breath.

Go to the Jewish market on 137th Street.

Padric studied the list as he walked. He decided which items he could lop off the list by slipping into his coat pocket. He passed the German bakery, then the vegetable shop. He helped himself to a small potato from the stand on the sidewalk. Suddenly there was a big commotion. Someone yelled at him. It was the owner, an aproned guy with yellow, wrinkly skin and glasses, a careworn face. The guy started to run after him. Padric ran like hell, around the corner, up an alleyway.

After catching his breath in the alleyway he realized he'd lost the ten-dollar bill. He was terrified out of his mind.

Mickey will kill me.

He realized that he'd better run away. But he had no money, just the oilcloth shopping bag and the half-eaten raw potato. Would Mary protect him from Mickey?

She didn't. Mickey went berserk and kicked him from room to room.

Padric wanted to get Free Lunch at school. A big blond Free Lunch Lady with brown stockings looked him up and down.

She told him, You can't. It's for poor children only.

I'm poor.

Are you on Home Relief?

I think so.

Bring a paper that says so and I'll put you on Free Lunch.

Under his breath he hissed, Go fry an egg.

After school he went into the box where Mary kept papers and pictures. He looked at the photo of himself at his First Holy Communion, in blue suit, knickers, long black stockings, white collar and bow tie with a white satin armband. He found a paper with red seals and gold letters that appeared as if it must be very important.

He took it to show the Free Lunch lady. She looked at it.

It's not the right paper. Take it right home.

A kid was reading the paper over her shoulder.

It's your Birth Certificate dummy, you're a bastard.

This reminded him of the first day of registration for school.

Ma, why isn't my last name on this paper? he'd asked her.

The paper's too small, she told him.

He waited for Mary at home, put the paper with red seals in her lap.

Am I a bastard?

Yes.

Who's my father?

A Welsh seaman, William Jones, who never knew he'd knocked me up. I was 15.

Padric always though that Mary shaved her age a bit in later years and might have been a few years older.

Mary taught Padric how to sew on her second-hand Singer machine. Quickly he showed affinity for sewing. He coveted Mary's sewing box that contained a tape measure, a tracing wheel, tailors chalk, a bent shears, a scissors, thread, needles, a tin thimble, a pincushion. He drew street scenes with the blue tailor's chalk on butcher paper.

Maybe you'll end up a tailor?

At ten he began to play with a boy who was very big and seemed strong. The boy was maybe sixteen, ugly and dumb, big and strong and masculine. Mary called him a "bad boy." His name was Joey Rust, he lived on Brook Avenue, had a reedy voice. They flipped cards against the wall, shouted "heads" or "tails."

Joey was famous for cheating at cards. Padric caught him, slapped him across the face.

Joey went after him. Padric ducked into his building and ran up four flights to Mary and hid behind her hips.

The next day, Joey laid for Padric and beat him up. Padric cried and screamed.

The day after Joey cornered him, I have a new game to play, don't be scared and don't try to guess.

He led Padric into the cellar of his building that smelled of heating oil, ice and wood.

Lay down next to that pile of firewood!

He did, pressing his face against the wall. He felt cold concrete against his warm cheek. Joey pulled down his pants, and made Padric cry when he stuck his big prick into his rectum. Slowly Padric stopped crying, he liked it.

From then on Joey and Padric fucked everywhere—on the roof, way above the clotheslines that crossed the inner courtyard. In one apartment or another when no one was around. Behind the stairway.

Once Joey raised his large legs up into the air.

Do it to me now.

Padric tried but since he didn't get hard, he couldn't do it right.

Uncle Johnny kept a girlie magazine in the toilet. Padric read: *Oh Venus of the world, thy lovely swelling titties, you lovely cock melter. Oh God, how many wet dreams have you caused me Fernando. Fernando not only kissed her but put his tongue into her mouth and while she enjoyed sucking it his hand crept up beneath her silken petticoats, till it felt her pouting cunnie. Señor Fernando threw up his silk pajamas, exposing his erect cock he separated her lovely thighs. Oh Marie, I love you so. He drew her hand down and made her clasp his manly pride.*

Padric was crazy about sex. Word got around the Bronx.

Next Padric tagged after Sonny Reilly, a skinny kid who smelled like pee. If Padric had some money, Sonny would go around with him. Sonny's family was poor. The grandparents, parents and kids all lived together in an apartment nearby that smelled bad and had an outdoor toilet with spiders in it.

Padric met Sonny on a Sunday afternoon after Mass. He had money, took Sonny to the movies, bought him soda and candy. The next Sunday Padric had no money.

Sonny made an ugly face.

I don't want to have nothing to do with you if you don't have no money.

Sonny walked away.

The entire neighborhood thrilled when the cops found Richard "Bruno" Hauptmann who kidnapped the Lindbergh baby on East Tremont Avenue in the Bronx. A mob gathered outside his house on East 222nd Street shouting, Bruno the Baby Killer! Burn him!

Padric read in the *Bronx Home News* that Bruno claimed a friend gave him a box to hold when the friend went back to Germany. Bruno explained that when he was repotting a snake plant he used the box for spilled dirt and found $14,000 in cold cash.

Padric asked Mary, What if it's true?

He's a dirty foreigner. You'll see, he'll burn.

A Jewish carpenter, Saul, gave Padric a dollar for sex. Also a soft buttered onion roll.

An Italian taxicab driver from around the corner gave him a nickel for a bottle of soda afterwards.

On a summer day while swimming in the filthy East River, Padric dove deep under the water and came up between someone's legs. That someone was a big blond boy, about eighteen or nineteen, named Walter. Walter took him to a rooming house where he lived by himself and held a pair of sharp scissors to Padric's head, pulled a red boner out from his swim trunks.

Suck it.

Padric did.

Every time they saw each other, Walter and Padric would go to the rooming house that reeked of cooked cabbage and Walter would grab the scissors.

Suck it.

There was a garage mechanic who walked his Alsatian dog by the marsh beside the river where Padric swam. They did it.

There was the grown son of the superintendent of the building around the corner, a Czech. He would take Padric's hand, put it on his prick.

Pull it, you dope.

Padric did.

Afterwards, they walked down the street and around the corner. The Czech boy bought two nickel bags of French fries. He kept one for himself and gave one to Padric. Padric added vinegar and salt to his. They sat on the stoop and ate every last French fry, greedily licked their fingers afterwards.

There was the super of Padric's building on Willis Avenue who led him down to the basement. He corn-holed Padric beside the furnace. He gave nothing afterwards.

Whenever Padric got money he bought himself some raw hamburger and ate it with his fingers behind the stairway. Sometimes he sliced up a raw potato and ate it with the raw chopped meat.

Steuben Beach had a pavilion. After a swim, he left the beach, wanting to listen to music and watch the (mostly) German people dance in the pavilion. "Mein Blonder Matrose" was the favorite song that summer. A stocky forty-year-old German baker named Fred bought Padric a ginger ale. He invited him to his home on Melrose Avenue to meet his daughter who was named Hannah. Fred lived with his sister Eva because his wife had died. Eva cared for Hannah and cooked and cleaned for Fred.

After that Fred would pick Padric up in his car at school at lunch hour. He'd take him home. He'd hand him a small beer stein that was filled to the brim with Schnapps. He was urged to drink the Schnapps even though he though it was horrible and bitter and burned while going down his throat. Once the stein was empty, Fred would demand a blow job or would fuck Padric. The first time he fucked him, Padric had his first orgasm.

On days when Fred's house wasn't empty, Fred would drive to the park, lock the car doors, roll up the windows, and smoke a cigar while Padric gave him a blow job.

Fred handed him a dollar each time.

Fred was also hot for Mary.

One day at Fred's house Padric noticed that Fred stored dollar bills in the sugar bowl on the kitchen table. After each visit Padric took one or two crumpled dollar bills until Fred caught him, and that was the end of Fred.

Playing hooky: Padric stole two nickels from Mary's purse. He took the IRT to the Bronx Zoo, spent the whole day wandering from the Yak House toward the Bear Den. When it started to drizzle he stayed inside a cedar shelter with the raccoons until it stopped. Finally, rushing through the Bear Den because the bears were dull, he spent the rest of the day in the Reptile House fixating on bloodsucking bats until it began to get very dark outside and he took the subway home, scared out of his mind that he'd get off at the wrong stop in the dark.

Playing hooky: Padric stole nickels from Mary's purse. He took the subway to Battery Park. He got the boat that went to the Statue of Liberty. He joined the tourists and climbed up the hundred or so flights of curling steps to the crown, and when he looked out across the water he could see land. He thought he lived in the direction of the land.

But then someone said, That's Brooklyn, stupid.

Playing hooky: Padric took the subway to Coney Island. He walked up Surf Avenue. At Steeplechase he tried the Earthquake Stairway, the Barrel of Love, the Whichaway. He liked Coney Island but the subway ride was much too long from the Bronx.

He helped Mary shell peas. They sat at the kitchen table.

Mama, I've got something to tell you. I'm a homosexual.

What's that?

Well, I like men. I like to wear girls clothes sometimes. I like makeup. I like to make love to men.

That's silly. It's a silly phase you're passing through. Now don't come home with any diseases!

Guess what Padric.

What?

Joey Rust's been sent to Reform School.

Aunt Rose died of alcoholism.

Padric stole from the crazy old German woman upstairs.

Padric stole from a young Italian couple in the next building.

Padric lit the ranges for two old Jewish couples on Friday night, the Sabbath, when Jews weren't allowed to light a match themselves. Those old Jews patted his head, gave him a few pennies during the week. He stole whatever he could find up there.

He stole a piggy bank—a dog with a wobbly head— from two small cousins.

Aunt Betty took him out to Flushing Meadows to the World's Fair. Everything was orange and blue. Futurama was the strangest exhibit. It let him glimpse into the future, see highways to far-away places high up in the air. He soaked up sunshine.

How come you got such big feet and hands, Paddy boy?

She smelled his breath.

You have nice breath, Paddy lad.

Thanks Aunt Betty.

Don't drink too much milk. It'll give you sour smelling breath. Don't eat fat, it will make your breath bitter. You'll know when your liver is bad because your breath will smell fishy.

He didn't do his homework, wouldn't listen when the teacher spoke. He was hungry, was waiting for lunch. He got left back when he was in seventh grade. Everyone else was thirteen or fourteen. He was over six feet tall, had to begin the seventh grade from the beginning again.

He got expelled from junior high for being incorrigible. Also, for playing hooky and cornholing in the gym shower.

Mary took him downtown to City College. He took an eight-hour test. He tested with an I.Q. of one hundred twenty-six.

The evaluator looked over the results of his tests.

You're not a moron. You're not retarded.

Padric was sent to a vocational training school to learn woodworking. The school was on the Lower East Side of Manhattan. He had to learn to transfer subway trains at Grand Central. When he broke the school's rules he got his ass paddled over a workbench. He went for a few weeks, didn't like wood, didn't like the tools, didn't like the sweaty smells, didn't like the teachers.

Harold was a redheaded man about thirty who smelled like ladies' powder. Harold was from the Bronx. They first had sex in Pelham Bay Park while mosquitoes ate both of them alive, and fireflies glowed, appeared, disappeared, never in one place.

Harold took Padric to the movies on Forty-Second Street. He took him to the Automat that had golden coffee spigots.

Harold told him, Workers of the world won't unite.

It was June 1941.

Then he revealed, There are lots of boys around here who like to play around with men.

He pointed out some of these boys. Padric's heart swelled, he felt like he belonged there. At home he was always wrong, terrified of Mickey, was known as "Sissy Mary" in the neighborhood. On Forty-Second Street were people like himself.

One hobunk on the fourth floor sat at the open window in his undershirt, singing:

> *Paddy has a nickel,*
> *Paddy wants a pickle*
> *Sissy Mary Paddy*

Summer of 1941: Padric stood on Forty-Second Street near Eighth Avenue. His knees were shaking. He saw someone who was referred to as Miss Scarlet by a gentleman in a captain's hat.

Miss Scarlet was manly-nelly and immediately glommed onto Padric as soon as he set eyes on him.

I'm a Florida farm boy girl, he explained, Call me "she" please.

Miss Scarlet was tall, frail, slightly oriental-looking, had a sister who was a lesbian. Padric had never met a real lesbian. Miss Scarlet had silky white skin and dark hair. Her real name was Philip van Breckinridge. Miss Scarlet was really street-wise even though she was only about seventeen.

She explained: Let me drum this into your thick Irish head. Men are Johns. Never go with one unless he promises money. Here's how to bargain... Here's how to settle...

From then on they charged tricks five, three and ten, or whatever they could get. Scarlet didn't approve of stealing from Johns. At that point Padric didn't know he could.

Padric kept the money he earned under his mattress in the Bronx. He was sixteen, had a good, tall body, a pretty face framed by thick auburn hair, a good line of blarney, an ample round ass. On Forty-Second Street he was the new kid on the block and quickly sold his ass.

Pretty soon all the Johns began to look alike. The Lust Look, Miss Scarlet called it.

Have you tried the new Lust Look, Ladies? You take semen, and pat it gently into your pores!

He hadn't known Miss Scarlet long when he met Miss Jackie Robinson. Within a few days Miss Scarlet and Miss Robinson asked him if he'd move in with them and share the rent in their East Thirties tenement railroad flat because he was quick-witted and cute.

Padric stopped sleeping in the Bronx, but didn't move out.

The new place had only two beds, but they managed, squeezed in two at a time sometimes. They slept all day, hustled all night. It was supposed to be Miss Robinson's apartment, she was a dirty old man of twenty-two.

Padric had four Johns one night. He got twenty dollars total. He bought Mary a jingly gold bracelet.

At the bars on Forty-Second Street Padric drank beer or sweet wine and ginger ale. One night a John offered him gin. He tried it. It heightened and brightened. He got prettier, talked wittier, attracted the next John with one flutter of his lashes.

September 1941. Miss Scarlet and Padric and two black queens were standing in a doorway on 8th Avenue. They were laughing and screaming, having a high old time. A guy in a loud sports shirt with pimples and a fat face, approached.

Miss Scarlet asks in her deepest magnolia drawl, Hello honey, ya'll need any help?

Yeah sister, you just come right along with me, and your girlfriend too, and you two colored queens too.

The cop took the four of them to City Prison, into the South Annex and dumped them into the cell that held the junkies. The cell was so cold, with only Miss Scarlet's big prick to keep him warm.

They were held there for two weeks.

Padric and Miss Scarlet sat in the courtroom. The swinging door opened. Mary came in. She strode down the aisle wearing a tailored charcoal suit (called a dressmaker's suit), that Padric had picked out for her a couple of years before and looked pretty good in himself, though it hung because he had smallish hips. Mary wore a white blouse under it, a little black bow at the throat, a black Robin Hood hat that sported a feather. Her auburn hair was slicked back under it. She wore very little makeup.

The vice cop read out the charges.

Mr. Breckinridge and Mr. McGarry are guilty of blocking a public doorway, disorderly conduct, disturbing the peace.

The judge asked Mary two questions: Why does your son call himself by a girl's name? Why does he like to wear girl's clothes and makeup?

What's wrong with that, Your honor? When I was a girl, I liked to wear boys clothes.

The Judge looked weary.

Miss Scarlet turned scarlet.

To tell the truth, Your Honor, I don't know what to do with him. These days he comes home all hours of the night and recently he doesn't come home at all. He won't go to work. They don't want him in school. Sometimes he has money that I don't know where he gets it from. I can't understand him, your honor. I've tried my best.

The judge looked directly at Mary.

Well, Missus, if you can't take care of your son, we'll do it for you.

He banged the gavel.

Two pen indefinite sentences in the reformatory.

Miss Scarlet was seventeen years old, Padric was sixteen.

Pen indefinite: A prisoner could do anywhere from six months to a maximum of three years on a pen indef while they were rehabilitating him. And then, parole for three years.

Officially, Padric and Miss Scarlet were too young for City Prison, so they were sent to Boys' Reformatory. They were put into isolation cells with solid steel doors, but no bars. They were put far from the other boys because they were queer. Their cells were side-by-side, a screen between. They could see each other but couldn't touch.

The warden came to see Padric. He brought books for him to read. Young boys began passing notes to Padric under the steel door. Also notes to Miss Scarlet.

One read: *Please sing, we want to hear your girly voices.*

There were six or seven little holes at the bottom of both of their doors. Padric and Scarlet would get naked and lie on their bellies on the floor, and see out at the other boys who would also lie down on the floor and peek in at them. Some of the boys kissed Padric's finger-tips through the holes.

After two weeks, Padric began visiting a psychiatrist. The psychiatrist knew all about the note passing and about the finger kissing.

You'll get in trouble, he warned. It's best that I put you in another institution with your own kind. Don't you agree?

I agree.

Padric and Miss Scarlet were put in a closed panel truck and taken to the Homo Block in City Prison.

All the homos on the Homo Block were adults. They were the only boys except for Miss Angel, a Puerto Rican kid who had been arrested for soliciting in drag. Miss Angel was thirteen and had syphilis. She was small and slim. They were known as "queens."

Padric guessed that's when he became a "queen." He didn't know for a while that "queen" only meant "homosexual" not that he was regal.

"Homosexual" was stamped on his records even though he'd been convicted of disorderly conduct. The theory was that "homos" are less trouble when kept together in one cellblock.

That record followed him around. It meant that he was segregated with queens in every prison where he did time, except the last one in California, and the two federal pens, years later.

Prison was just like Forty-Second Street except there were no cars and taxis or movie theaters. Padric got friendly with every "girl" in the Homo Block:

Sweet Sue from the Bronx.

Goldola, sixty if she was a day.

Gigi.

Miss Mattie Dears.

The Jersey Lily.

Miss Bondey who could sing "Some of These Days" just like Sophie Tucker.

Miss Maybe, a sweet black queen who got famous later.

Fat Blindeens who had only one eye, and only liked to go with uncircumcised men.

Kitty Cunt who was reputed to turn between forty and fifty tricks each night near the Brooklyn Navy Yard, at $1 each.

She explained, I get myself *arranged*. I'd lay up in a room, serve cunt. Those seamen can't tell the difference.

Gorgeous Junkie Chuck.

Mickey Rapucci, a thief who Padric fell for.

Mama Sutton, a madam from Brooklyn connected with the famous scandal involving several senators that got into the papers.

A queen from New Mexico. Padric also loved her, but never remembered her name.

Scrap Iron Mae West, a muscular queen missing many teeth, but with metal replacement teeth.

Miss Kitty Darling, a Jewish drag queen whose father owned a kosher chicken restaurant in Brooklyn.

Clara Bow with red hair

Clara Bow with blond hair.

Greta Garbo, whom Padric knew from Forty-Second Street.

Miss Katie Hepburn, a black "girl" who would sometimes be so desperate she'd do it for five cents.

Kay Francis, a Swedish muscle-bound queen who looked like a longshoreman.

Christmas: Padric was sixteen. His entire block was moving boulders across a big field. It began to snow. Padric began to cry. Miss Francis noticed the tears, pressed Padric's head against her flat chest and crushed him with her big, brawny arms covered with tattoos. Padric sobbed but he didn't know why.

Miss Francis crooned, There, there honey. It won't always be this bad.

All winter they moved dirty boulders. Miss Scarlet, Miss Angel, Padric, and all the "girls."

Spring: The Homo Block residents were outfitted with big straw hats. They became farmerettes, tilling the big fields all day, segregated from the "real" boys who worked the machine shop, mess hall, bakery, and the other jobs that kept the prison functioning. In the fields the "girls" planted asparagus, tomatoes, turnips, strawberries, radishes, beets. Padric hoed, discovered how things grew.

At dawn the entire Homo Block filed into the fields and worked all day.

Sometimes Padric was sent back into the prison because they needed an extra worker. He was told to unload sacks of flour, sometimes coal. He'd tie a handkerchief over his hair to keep off the coal dust and flour. He didn't mind this work at all because he could score fresh bread from the bakery when it came out hot with buckets of molasses and coffee. He became strong. Quite quickly he could carry one hundred pound sacks on each of his shoulders.

He would sneak off into the tool shed with another queen or one of the boys from the barn. Because he was sixteen, very "chicken," he was in big demand. Miss Scarlet told him that his admirers were known as "chicken queens."

After taking Padric down to the clinic for some shots, one of the guards put him on the big scale to weigh him, and—when nobody was looking—kissed him directly on the mouth. On his way out of the clinic, Padric passed a long line of entirely naked straight men.

The guard whispered in his ear, The time of year for syphilis shots.

Padric shrugged.

The guard told him, You wouldn't slough it off so easy if a big dilator was stuck into your urethra to break up your adhesions.

Every once in a while Mary wrote a line or two or visited.

Once Padric went into the visiting room where Mickey was waiting, smelling like fish, a swatch of pus-soaked gauze stuck to the back of his neck where a fat boil was ripening.

Stay out of trouble while you're here, he instructed. Mary and I will help you be good when you get out. We'll go to the Polo Grounds.

Padric and Miss Scarlet made plans to go down south together.

The north country is inhospitable to a gently bred
Southern belle like me, Miss Scarlet explained.

But, I'll be on parole when I get out. I'll have to live
with Mary and Mickey, be a good little normal teenager.

The parole date was nearing. On a Saturday afternoon
an interview with a psychiatrist was scheduled. The other
girls had gone to the farm without him. He was all alone
in the Homo Block. The radio was pouring out "Madame
Butterfly" and he sang along at the top of his voice.

Up the stairs from the Bing, the punishment cellblock
on the tier below the Homo Block, came a two hundred
fifty pound ape with a protruding belly, an Irish face not
unlike Mickey's, with hanging earlobes, donkey's ears—a
Neanderthal in a blue uniform—Mr. Rawlins. Padric saw
Rawlins waddling up the stairs, like the monster out of
H.G. Wells *Time Machine*, a creature that lived under the
earth.

He was in the middle of *Un bel di vedremo.*

Who the hell is making all that noise?

Me, Sir.

Whatthehell you think you're doing?

Rawlins swung his fist at Padric and missed.

Get the hell downstairs, faggot.

He turned and began to descend the steel steps. Rawlins kicked at him once so he would move faster. He was
trembling because Rawlins terrified him. He ran down
the stairs, Rawlins close behind him.

When they got down to the Bing, Rawlins pushed him
against the grill fence.

He told him, Strip down to your shorts.

Rawlins went into his little office and Padric could hear him dialing the telephone. Three hacks arrived through the door that led out to the central desk. He was shocked that one was an albino blond.

This fag thinks he can sing.

The hacks started punching him and pushed him back and forth from one to the other. One hit him in the hip and chest, another kicked him in the leg calf. One pounded his back and the back of his neck. Padric started screaming pretty loud.

In the tier above, the queens were returning from the fields. They heard him screaming.

They started screaming too, Let her alone, let her alone. She's just a kid you big apes.

The sound of forty screaming queens was one helluva racket, like a pack of caged monkeys.

The beating stopped when he slithered down to the cement floor and lay there sobbing.

One hack told him, Shut up.

He stopped, tried to get up but Rawlins wouldn't let him get up, had his big foot on his chest.

Rawlins told him, Crawl.

So he rolled over and crawled on his hands and knees. Rawlins nudged him around the corner of the stairs, kicked his ass into a cell in the Bing on the right. Later, Rawlins threw in a blanket, also a pair of felt slippers. Soon Rawlins went home and the night guard came on.

The night guard told him, Don't worry, nothin' terrible is going to happen to you.

But Padric was very frightened, wanted to go back upstairs to be with the other girls.

In the morning Rawlins held "court."

Stand up there, McGarry, put your hands behind your back.

He read off the charge: Creating a disturbance in the cellblock.

Guilty.

Sentence: Five days on bread and water in the Dark Bing. Ten days added to your sentence.

Rawlins put him into the Dark Bing, a totally dark cell.

You goddam queer, you're not Irish. There are no Irish queers!

Yes Sir.

The first three days in the dark were horrible. He had nothing to smoke, was terribly hungry. He tried to sleep as much as possible. He tried to remember all the songs Aunt Betty used to sing when she was drunk. There was a faucet next to the toilet, so he did have water. Three times a day two slices of white bread were slipped under the door.

Every day Rawlins would shout at him, You goddamn queer, you're not Irish. There are no Irish queers!

On the fifth day he was let out and sent back to the Homo Block. Right away he was transferred to a new cell, in a new location. This was routine when someone got out of punishment. He was pretty weak after five days on bread and water and was half-carried up to his new cell on the fifth tier by Kay Francis and Jersey Lily who made up his bed, lit and put a cigarette between his lips. When he took a drag, he almost fell on the cement floor, was so knocked out by the smoke. Kay Francis caught him. His mouth tasted bitter, also metallic. His teeth were coated with fur.

You got to eat to make up for your time down there. Remember you're a growing girl.

Kay Francis took him aside, Miss Scarlet O'Hara left while you were in the Bing. She went back down south on parole, asked me to say goodbye to you. She'll write to you.

His seventeenth birthday passed without notice.

He was released on parole in September, was instructed to go home to Mary's new apartment, given a long list of parole instructions.

He skimmed the instructions:

Parolee must abstain from using intoxicating liquors and shall not frequent places where they are sold... He shall avoid disreputable associations and cheerfully obey the law and conduct himself at all times as a good citizen...

Mary, Mickey and his half sisters, Elizabeth and Jeanne, had moved away from the Bronx while he was in prison. Mary and Mickey had become building superintendents in Washington Heights.

The prison gave him a suit and a few dollars. He was released and got on the IRT Broadway-Seventh Avenue subway wanting to go to 157th Street but got lost. He didn't know Washington Heights. He found himself outside a wooded, hummocky cemetery. He walked a bit, then asked a man in front of a building that had a brass plaque stating "The Museum of the American Indian" for directions.

He thought he was following the directions but found himself facing the Fort Lee cliffs of the Palisades and tan high-rise structur es with large windows, a pyramidal series of buildings, obviously a massive hospital.

Finally he found Mary and Mickey's apartment. It was around the corner from Mother Cabrini High School on Fort Washington Avenue. The supers' apartment was in the basement, so he went down the dark, stinky stairway. Mary was at home and Mickey was at work. Padric sat at the white kitchen table with Mary. It was the same table from the Bronx. He wore the suit they'd given him in prison. He ate baloney and mayonnaise sandwiches.

I'm going to settle down. I promise I'll stay out of trouble.

He meant it.

The window in Mary's kitchen was below ground, below a grate. Light rays and muffled sounds of passing people, trucks changing gears, sirens, came through the grate.

Mary warned him, We're supposed to tell you that parole is only a conditional release under supervision, not unconditional release without supervision. Get it? Mickey and I will supervise you. Get it?

Padric asked, Is there more baloney?

No.

Liverwurst?

No.

Spam?

No.

He spread mayonnaise on slices of bread. It made a fine sandwich.

Mary warned him: Don't be so sarcastic. I mean it.

Padric's dream: He finds sixty thousand dollars in small bills in a satchel. He buys Mary a house. He buys Elizabeth and Jeannie clothes, bracelets, pays for a dentist to fix all their teeth. Mickey is no longer in the picture.

On the first visit, Padric's parole officer kept his hands straight out across the desk, covering a pile of folders.

Why don't you try to get a job as an office boy in the place that your aunt works?

Aunt Rose had died of alcoholism while he was in the can. The other aunt, Aunt Betty, had a good job at a big mail order company in downtown Manhattan.

He went to the personnel office at Aunt Betty's office building and got an interview with the personnel man. He sat stiffly, hands in his lap.

My aunt is Mrs. Betty Watson who works here.

After the interview he went to see Betty at her desk.

Hello Aunt Betty.

There were rows of filing cabinets along the wall. Rose looked up from an adding machine, turned the swivel chair toward him. The tip of her nose was pink.

Hello Patty.

That night Betty came all the way up to Washington Heights. Padric, Mary and Betty gathered in a little room in the back of the apartment.

Are you a homosexual, she asked?

No.

He began to cry. Betty was mad as hell but didn't say anything else. She slammed out of the apartment.

Addictions in the family:

Padric: raw hamburger, anything made with potatoes

Elizabeth: raw potatoes

Jeanne: vanilla extract

The new year, 1943: A ring around the moon.

Mickey told him: I went to Forty-Second Street one time and got my prick sucked by some queen who stole my wallet.

Mickey laughed so hard he farted twice.

Padric thought: I wish it was me that robbed you. Me that sucked you off.

He hated and desired Mickey. At night he spied on Mickey when he'd go to the bathroom, trying to find out what kind of equipment he had but he never could because Mickey wore such baggy drawers. He decided that it mustn't be much because Mary always said, Mickey isn't much good as a man, he's just a good provider.

He looked for a job as an office boy (junior clerk) at *Esquire Magazine*. He got it. He tried not to swish but what he really wanted to do was go down south and join Miss Scarlet.

He lasted twenty-four days at the magazine.

Miss Scarlet wrote regularly.

*Y'all come on down and live with me! I got me a second-hand
car. It's got a red stripe around the middle, it's a Ford convertible
phaeton with whitewall tires and genuine cow leather seats.*

But Padric couldn't leave New York without permission from his parole officer.

Once a week he went downtown to the parole officer.
Is everything okay Pat?
Yeah
You staying out of trouble?
Yeah.
See you next week.
He didn't tell him he'd already lost his magazine job
for dropping a pile of manuscripts that he was supposed
to deliver from the ninth floor to the eighth.

Elizabeth shared her cache of russets. Padric peeled
and sliced over newspaper. They shared the raw slices
with shakes of salt. He made Elizabeth laugh.

Mickey kept a pint of brandy hidden in the back of
the coat closet. Padric found it, swiped it. He hid the
pint in a Klein's shopping bag under some clothes that
his half-sisters had outgrown. Two or three times a day
he went into the closet, took a sip of brandy, or two sips.
The taste was awful, it made him gag. The closet smelled
like musty wool. Quickly he went into the bathroom and
drank a chaser of water, then washed his mouth out with
Sen-Sen.

When he looked, he realized that the bottle was empty and bought another pint. And another.

Padric wandered back down to Times Square. The Johns were there as they always were, but Miss Scarlet was missing. He walked into Bryant Park off Forty-Second Street and Sixth Avenue behind the big library with two stone lions in front on Fifth Avenue. He hustled up a few dollars.

He took his Johns to a third-rate hotel on Eighth Avenue that the hustlers called Tillie's Whorehouse. Tillie's charged $3.50 for a room, and gave kickbacks, usually $1. Sometimes he rented the same room three or four times on the same night.

One night after he had already earned $22, after drinking all day too, he decided to call it a night and go out to eat at an all-night coffee shop on Eighth Avenue. It was about 3 o'clock in the morning,.

A seedy, paunchy guy waddled up the avenue. He walked right up to him and showed him a lady's gold watch.

It's a 21-jewel Lady Hamilton.

So?

I don't have any money but I'll give you the watch if you go with me.

He wanted the watch like crazy. Mary would love it.

Okay. But you gotta be quick.

He took the guy to Tillie's, to one of the little rooms. He sat on the bed with the John, then blacked out.

He woke. Pinkish dawn glowed along Eighth Avenue. The John was gone. He put his hand into his pocket. His $22 was gone. The John hadn't even left him carfare home.

He looked into the window of a diner on Tenth Avenue. He saw Miss Greta Garbo, one of the queens from the Homo Block. She was having breakfast. He barged in, sat down, told her his sad story.

She pushed a nickel across the Formica.

I'll stake you to a subway ride.

Dip work:

He knelt in front of a John in a hallway on Eighth Avenue. He sucked like crazy. At the same time he went through every pocket of the guy's trousers with his hands, also his coat pockets. He hugged and pulled and jerked the guy well, giving sensational head work. The John thought that the motion was passion. He was concentrating on coming. He was drunk. Padric found his wallet in the back pocket and palmed it. The man came, immediately staggered away.

A grey-haired John, not drunk, wanted a blow-job. Padric took him into a hallway on Eighth Avenue.

Pay me first.

The John handed him $3, then opened his fly.

No. Drop your pants. I want to kiss you all around, honey, you're so gorgeous, I really want to love you good.

The John dropped his pants, his shorts. The grey-flannel pants pooled around his ankles. Padric gave a sensational performance with his head. Meanwhile his fingers opened the John's wallet, removed the bills, slipped the wallet back in. The John ejaculated. Padric was on his feet, out in the street like a gazelle. The John took a minute, leaned against the wall, then reached down and pulled up his shorts, then his pants. He zipped up his fly.

He went home with a Greek cook. The cook's apartment was around the corner from the terra cotta and brick Broadway Tabernacle at Fifty-Sixth Street. There was a colored icon of Jesus and Mary on the wall of his room. All over the floor, around the bed, were sheets of tissue paper. The cook also had twine running from the headboard to the footboard of the bed. The tissue paper crinkled when they walked over it and they had to slide under the string to get into the bed. The cook put his wallet under the pillow, was very drunk. He reached up his arms.

Sega, sega. That's slowly, slowly in Greek.

After sex, the cook passed out. Padric took the bills out of the wallet, then put back the wallet. With the bills in his mouth he slid out from under the twine onto the tissue paper, tippy-toeing like Margot Fonteyn on his bare feet over the papered area to the bare floor. He got dressed. The Greek snored. He grabbed the Greek's trousers and took them onto the landing. He found a gold cigarette case, pocketed it and threw the trousers back into the room.

Another night, with a fresh buzz on, he turned right onto Forty-Second Street from Seventh Avenue. A big hand grabbed him. The Greek cook put a two-pronged fork to his head.

My gold cigarette case!

What case?

Don't lie to me.

I gave it to my mother in Washington Heights. I'll go uptown and get it for you. I'm sorry. I must have been drunk. I don't usually do things like that...

The cook wasn't buying this.

Padric kicked his long leg like a chorus girl, smacked the cook under the jaw and ran like hell.

Greta Garbo told him: You got to keep changing your hustling territory. Never take anything but the green.

Padric led a young sailor into a gloomy hallway painted two shades of dark green. The sailor was sloshed. He pushed the sailor up against the wall, went down on his knees, he sucked him like crazy and finger-fucked him at the same time. With his other hand he got at his wallet, emptied out the money and returned it to the sailor's back pocket.

Later he counted the money, $108, a bulls-eye.

Just before dawn, after drinking and eating on Eighth Avenue, he was walking (not steadily) down Eighth Avenue toward the subway. Eight sailors, an entire Conga number like a scene from *My Sister Eileen*, came toward him.

That's him! There he is! Kick his balls in!

He took off down the avenue; he was very fast and got away.

He took Garbo's advice worked other neighborhoods:

West 72nd Street

Third Avenue in the 50's

The Village.

Bryant Park.

I'll have a Coke, he told the bartender in an East Side club.

After turning tricks in other parts of town, he liked to end up in Times Square in order to eat macaroni and cheese—crispy on top, creamy inside—at the Automat at Park Avenue and Forty-Second Street. Sometimes he treated himself to two or three orders. Queens he knew fluttered in to drink brown coffee that poured out of gold spigots.

He rode on an open bus up Fifth Avenue to Central Park, stood at the fountain and looked at the Plaza Hotel.

A winter night, early in 1943: Padric sashayed past a fur store in the 30's near Seventh Avenue. He was sloppy drunk, sorry for himself. He had a knot in his stomach as hot as a glowing ember. He remembered what Miss Jersey Lily had taught him in prison: You pick out a store window that's on a quiet street, not near a busy one. You pick out what is most hockable. You toss a brick through the window, grab the item, run like hell to a busy street, lose yourself in a crowd. Easy!

He looked into the window of the fur store. His eyes were drawn to a mink coat marked $800. He threw a brick through the window. The alarm sounded like fifty thousand alarms as he reached through the jagged glass, gashed his arm trying to make the hole larger. He grabbed the coat, ran like a bat out of hell up the deserted street.

Two cops saw him running, chased him in the car. They drove up onto the sidewalk, pinned him against a shop window. Blood poured down his arm.

The cops pushed him against the squad car. Searched every inch of his body.

He turned eighteen. He was brought into court by two guards.

The crime: Stealing a muskrat coat (it wasn't mink at all, it wasn't $800 either). The muskrat was worth $80. Larceny.

Sentence: Pen indef.

Back in the Homo Block. Padric rejoined the queens. There was much squealing and hugging. He met Bobby, a Norwegian queen, skinny, hair slicked back, a few dirty blond curls in front. She became his new friend.

At night after lights out, Bobby crooned loudly.

I have such lovely white skin! I do have such lovely white skin.

Bobby told him. I hate Negro people.

At lunch he sat beside Bobby. Miss Ivy, six foot four, three feet wide, cueball bald, soot black, came rushing up to greet him. She put her hand on Bobby's shoulder.

He shrieked out at Miss Ivy, Take your big black paw off me!

Miss Ivy did, real fast. Then Padric threw his arms around Miss Ivy's big body.

He sniveled, I'm sorry Miss Ivy.

That's all right child.

He cut Bobby dead, didn't finish lunch.

Some of the girls:

Lady Plushbottom, an African warrior with an over-size buttocks. Her husband was called The Black Prince. He was a second story man. Padric loved Lady Plushbottom's nipples.

Peaches from Belgium who could draw geisha girls with crayons on old white sheets.

Miss Eva Coo, sang "Estralita" in *coloratura* soprano.

JuJu Greene was a Jewish girl from Brooklyn.

JuJu told him, I have a python, a boa constrictor, five Pekinese dogs and a tank full of fish in my cold-water flat in Brooklyn. I'm afraid they'll all die while I'm locked up here.

Baroness Stephanie Hortense Evantee, a Baron of Swedish royalty, or so she claimed.

Miss Carol, a tiny but vicious platinum blond queen.

Lady Godiva who had no hair but wore a garish red wig to cover the baldness.

Roberta Hopseena, a high school teacher who knelt beside the bunk at night, clasped her hands together and intoned out loud, Now I lay me down to sleep I pray the lord my soul to keep if I should die before I wake I pray the lord my soul to take.

Miss Camille, the most beautiful girl in the world, had no control over her vomit. She was known to upchuck during conversation, in her sleep, with no notice when she did.

Miss Bianca Edith had the cell beside his. Miss Edith was slender, blonde, twenty-five. She was a quiet hero-in addict. Padric and the others tried to guess how Miss Edith managed to get drugs in prison. No one saw her score drugs, or shoot drugs, but she was stoned or on the nod all the time. For some reason, unknown to the rest of them, Miss Edith wasn't required to work on the farm, or anywhere in the prison like everyone else. When the others marched off to work, she sat in her cell, on the nod. No one ever saw her have a visitor either.

In the middle of one night, he heard Miss Edith scream, Motherfuck motherfuck motherfuck.

Miss Edith shouted the same thing over and over again. Motherfuck motherfuck motherfuck motherfuck motherfuck motherfuck.

Lights went on in the hall, people were running. But, because the walls between his cell and Miss Edith's was solid steel, there was no way to know what was happening.

The next morning Miss Edith's cell was empty. The word was that she was dead before they got her out of the cell. An overdose? Obviously.

Officially, it was a heart attack.

Home remedies Padric tried that were suggested by various girls:

nutmeg in water

mace

sniffing shellac

lighter fluid sniffing
shoe polish drained through white bread
"squeeze" – a colorless liquid, and ghastly
aspirins in Coke
aspirin in cigarettes
ginseng

Near the Homo Block was another block designated "Possible Homos." A "Possible Homo" was a man who had been apprehended in the act of inserting his penis into the mouth or anus of another man. His partner, the receiver of the male organ, was classified as "Homo" and put in with Padric and his kind.

Moe was a "Possible Homo" who was a trusty. He was the block clerk, and had the run of the place. Moe was making it with Miss Carol, until Miss Carol got paroled. Then Moe made up to Padric right away. Moe was pale and skinny. He had a pale skinny organ. He looked as though he always needed a shave. He and Moe had "parties" in his cell.

Moe bragged to a fat hack he knew, I have a new teenage girl-friend on the Homo Block. He does whatever I want.

In the middle of the night Padric was sound asleep. He was awakened when he heard his door clank open, saw a fat thing in a uniform by the light of a flashlight. He saw a badge, a gun, a fat prick hanging out of a fly. The hack grabbed his hand.

A wheezy voice announced, Curiosity killed the cat. But satisfaction brought him back.

The hack sure was ugly. He reminded him of Joey Rust. Padric bit him but gave him what he wanted.

He learned how to play bridge during his sentence. He usually played with Roberta Hopseena against Miss Kitty Cunt—still in prison from before—and Baroness Evantee. They played for a box of butter cookies from the commissary.

Kitty Cunt would slap her cards and trill, That card is good as a dick, honey, good as a dick.

He had a boyfriend named Johnny, a "Possible Homo" who once had gonorrhea, was proud of it.

Johnny explained, It shows prowess. You're not the only one, see.

The "Possible Homo" block was five tiers of cells directly above his, on "The Flats" or ground floor. During evening recreation hour, when all the cell doors were open, the prisoners were allowed to visit other prisoners on their own tier. Johnny and Padric would each go down to the back of their row, Johnny up on the fifth tier of cages, Padric on the flats. Padric would get one of the girls to act as a lookout, to flash him the sign that The Man had returned to his old barber chair at the front of the tiers, where he couldn't see anything unless he stood up.

Padric would swing up to the gallery of the first tier, lift himself up on a railing, then chin and climb like a monkey all the way up five tiers of cells. Johnny was waiting for him. Padric would drop his pants, get screwed right then and there with his head and arms hanging out over the abyss because it was a narrow walkway. He had to keep one eye down on the flats where the queens could see The Man and let him know if he moved from his barber chair. It wasn't great sex as sex, even jail sex, went. He did it (mostly) to put on a show and make the girls laugh and to show how strong and agile he was.

When they were done, Padric dropped straight down from tier to tier holding his hands out in front to break the fall. He swung down past each level.

Kitty Cunt told him during a bridge game, It's the most thrilling thing I ever saw. You scoot up those tiers like a human fly, then drop down, Miss Tarzana.

The name Miss Tarzana stuck.

Mary didn't visit during his eighteen month term. She wrote:

I've walked out on Mickey after 17 years. Elizabeth and Jeanne and me are living on the West Side of Manhattan in the 60's, Hell's Kitchen. It's a brownstone not far from a freight yard.

He was released in August of 1944. Since he was only nineteen, Mary was still responsible for him.

He was told, Go home to your mother.

Mary had a $32-a-month apartment. She was working on an assembly line in a war plant that manufactured military rucksacks. Elizabeth was fifteen and had a job too. Jeanne was eleven and went to school. Mary moved Jeanne into Elizabeth's room and gave Padric the little room that had been Jeanne's.

When Mary and Padric were alone she asked, Would you help me get rid of the child I'm carrying? I don't want my boyfriend at the plant to know.

He could never say no to her.

They picked a night when Elizabeth was out and Jeanne was having a sleep-away with a friend. He brought home a bottle of gin. Mary took a series of little black Eno pills and sat in a tub of scalding, hot water. Soon, Padric brought fresh mustard plasters, which he applied. She drank the gin, turned bright pink, waited for a miscarriage. She drank more gin. Waited, and soon ran more hot water, added water boiled on the stove and scalding. Mary's eyelids drooped, her skin turned lobster red and looked swollen.

Mary Jane was born seven months later. She was a beautiful Heidi. After a few weeks Mary adopted her out to a distant cousin.

Mary's friend on the same assembly line had a daughter named Kate Rose. The mothers put their heads together and decided to match up Padric and Kate Rose. Kate Rose was eighteen, he was nineteen. She was a cute Irish girl.

Mary told Kate Rose to walk into his room first thing in the morning. Kate Rose'd close the door, sit on his bed and wake him up. After a whole night of hustling, he could barely open his eyes. He felt her firm ass touching his head.

He did what he was told and went to the Bronx draft board to register for the draft. A gorgeous mulatto woman interviewed him. As soon as he met her he told her everything—about the Homo Block, about Rawlins. She had his file in front of her anyway.

Honey, I'm going to save you a lot of trouble. You won't even have to take a physical. I'm going to put you in 4-F right here and now.

You are? I think I might like the army. It sounds like prison but with more freedom. Food. A place to sleep. Regular guys...

Even though I think you're cute as a button, you'd officially be a detriment to the armed forces. Goodbye.

He met a queen at Bickfords on Eleventh and Broadway.

He and two other queens crossed Central Park on Halloween, 1944. Everyone was completely made up—lipstick, mascara, powder, the works—but wore boys' clothes. Also all were drunk and noisy.

They were arrested for "Disorderly Conduct."

On the record: "Sentence Suspended."

End 1944, early, cold 1945: A letter from Miss Scarlet O'Hara on eggshell-pink stationery was delivered:

You're the best girlfriend I've ever had. Why don't you come down south and live with me and my mother and my sister. It's warm here. You should really get away from that fright of a mother of yours...

Another letter from Miss Scarlet O'Hara:

Get on a bus and come on down south. We'll take a place together, work together, be good cruising-together sisters. Hustling's no good after you are twenty. It's time to give up pounding the pavements all night. It's an unlived life.

Letter from Miss Scarlet O'Hara:

We'll have lots of fun, lots of sex but we'll stay out of trouble. I have a job as a clerk in a drugstore. You can work in the same place if you like.

But he was on parole until 1946 and it was only March 1945.

As sweetly as he could, he asked his parole officer, Will you give me permission to leave the state?

No.

Please.

I might have if you weren't planning to live with another ex-convict. That's called an 'unhealthy association.'

Maybe making a big score would turn things around? He felt nothing special but for no reason tears purled down his cheeks.

On a cold evening in March he picked up a naval officer with two stripes on his sleeves. The officer was as drunk as anyone could be. He lurched up to Padric and started talking. Padric thought that he looked like he must be carrying at least fifty.

He tried to get him into a hallway. The officer balked. He tried to get him to the hotel. He refused. Padric was desperate and hailed a cab that took the officer over to Mary's place in Hell's Kitchen where Mary and the girls were asleep.

He bolstered the officer up and led him down the hall to his little bedroom. He helped the officer strip down to his drawers and stretched him across the bed. Padric could see he was passed out so he grabbed his wallet, emptied it. He counted $21. Hardly the haul he'd hoped for.

He sat down on the side of the bed. The officer snored. He could hear Mary breathing regularly next door. He thought of her as Mother Machree.

As amber dawn came up in New York he was on a bus passing the Jersey wetlands headed for Philadelphia.

He wondered what would become of Kate Rose? Will they bother to fix her up with someone else? Would Mary even give the officer a cup of coffee before she kicked him out of the apartment?

He felt weepy but held back.

He arrived in Philadelphia and found the famous baths he'd heard other queens tell about. He was in heaven. The baths had four large rooms in a row, each one darker than the one before, each packed full of army-style cots and writhing nude male bodies.

He slept in the baths.

The second day, cocktail hour, he found a gay bar where he met a businessman who drove him to an orgy/party in a house in Upper Darby, right outside the city limits. The house had three floors on which at least fifty men of various ages were spread out. The businessman introduced Padric to the host. He said Hi and made a beeline for the bar.

You brought *her*, you *fuck* her, he heard the host tell the businessman.

He had sex on every floor. Drunk, drunker, and drunk-est. Light as a floating feather.

He woke naked and alone on a couch in the living room, could hear voices coming from the kitchen. His underpants were inside his pants that were flung across a toppled vase of broken tulips. He stumbled into the kitchen. Two men turned to face him, smiling at the sight of him.

Was I okay?

You were the life of the party except you passed out cold. You voracious monster! Callow guest! We decided to let you sleep.

The two suburbanites lived together in Upper Dar-by. They had been together for many years but to avoid getting bored with each other they threw an orgy once a month. Padric looked around. He saw a big refrigerator. One of the guys opened it to get cream out and he no-ticed that it was loaded with food.

I wouldn't mind staying around here a while!

I'll stake you to train fare as far as Washington.

His hosts drove him to the train station; they sat in the front of the Ford, put Padric in the back seat. One of them slipped him $5 without the other knowing.

He was impressed by the grandeur of Union Station, Washington, D.C. He walked outside and saw the Capi-tol building. He remembered *Mr. Deeds Goes to Town* and thought about Jean Arthur and Gary Cooper, how funny they were. Why couldn't I be either a Jean OR a Gary? He thought about what it would be like if it was he who inherited twenty million dollars. Would Mary declare him insane? Would she lock him up to get his millions?

He went back into the station that was teeming with activity. Being wartime, men and women wore every imaginable uniform. He went into the "tearoom." At the next urinal stood an adorable sailor, maybe seventeen years old. This little bit of seafood was releasing a bright yellow frothing stream against the porcelain. They smiled and looked at each other, wanted sex but had nowhere to go and went back out into the Main Concourse together.

The sailor told him, I'm stationed here in Washington. Are you going somewhere?

Yes. I have a few days liberty, I'm on my way to my hometown in Georgia. Ours is a little town. My father is the sheriff there.

Well, I have a rich lover waiting for me down south. I'm on my way to live with him. But my money got stolen last night in Upper Darby outside of Phili.

The sailor bought them cheese sandwiches.

I wish I was the rich lover you were going to live with. When I get out of the Navy I'm going to go to New York or somewhere and be queer. That is if I don't get killed overseas.

They sat in the station until the sailor got on his night train for Georgia.

Padric left the station.

He asked a Redcap, Where is Lafayette Square?

It's across the street from the White House. You take a bus.

The Redcap told him which number bus.

He got off the bus nearby Lafayette Square, walked to the top step of the Jefferson Memorial to look at the White House for a while. He thought about President Franklin D. Roosevelt, so close by, probably sleeping alongside Eleanor.

He met a guy in the park who had owl-like, sly eyes. They guy took him to his house in a two-tone car. The weirdo wanted to have sex, but Padric was so tired he couldn't stay awake, and fell asleep.

In the morning the guy woke up early.

I got to go to work. You got to get out.

He ate at a Chinese restaurant and then checked into the YMCA on G Street. He found a bar, picked up a drunk who took him to a swanky apartment. The drunk gave him a Lucky Strike. They had sex, then the drunk passed out.

Immediately he got busy in the closet. He gathered together a couple of beautiful suits and overcoats. He dressed in the new clothes, left his old clothes neatly hanging in the closet that had sliding doors that he'd never before seen. He couldn't find a suitcase, so he just held the cache in his arms.

His arms were so loaded down, it was necessary to abandon a few pieces of clothing in the street where it was cold and icy. He carried what remained of the stash to the Y and checked out. He took a bus to the edge of the District of Columbia, stood on a highway heading south with about two dollars in his pocket and an armful of clothes in his arms.

He was lucky right away. A friendly salesman picked him up in a station wagon. The salesman had crimped eyes, a wedding ring.

The salesman stopped outside a small town in Virginia. The road was icy, treacherous.

I can't take you any further, this is where I live.

He blew the salesman in the station wagon by way of thanks.

I got to get on home, the salesman told him.

He gave him $5 and put him and his bundle out onto the slick highway. The sky looked like it was about to burst with new snow.

He gave some clothes to a black man who passed by. Because it was so cold he put the rest of the clothes on, a beautiful dark blue cashmere overcoat on top, the most beautiful coat he'd ever had on in his life—before or after. He was pretty miserable; it was homesickness. He was sorry he'd left Mary and the girls. Maybe it was the cold. He'd never felt anything remotely like that before. He guessed he was hungry too. He usually was.

He looked pretty funny wearing layers of jackets and coats. Very few cars came by and none stopped.

He lay in the frozen grass on the side of the road and sobbed.

Mama, Mama.

The stolen clothes were on his back and his skinny fruit body shook from head to toe. He was one miserable queen.

He heard, What's the matter, child?

An old, old black woman's face was looking down at him.

I seen you from my house. Didn't ya know yas in a colored area? What's the trouble, child?

He saw a house set a few yards back from the highway.

I'm a long way from home and I miss my mother. Could I sit in your house for a while and get warm?

I'd love to keep you there but you and I would be in trouble if the white folks saw me taking a white boy in my house.

She showed him where to go, and he waited out back of her house until she brought him something to eat— cold biscuits, some meat. He kept sniveling, was freezing, but stopped shaking and sobbing.

Richmond, Virginia.

He met a man named Sergeant Jack O'Kelly who said he was a sportswriter. He was also a chicken queen.

I cover baseball games and things for the newspaper on the Army base here. I'm on furlough.

Jack took him for a big dinner in a snazzy place in Richmond. Jack brought a bottle of good rum to the restaurant hidden in a brown paper sack. Set-ups were provided by the restaurant. Padric ate a full turkey dinner with all the trimmings, plus pecan pie, a taste new to him

Over stingers, Jack sighed deeply, Now you can suck my dick.

They spent the night together but Padric didn't re-member much because of all the rum. He did hear, as if it was coming from far away, the sound of someone running up or down a flight of metallic stairs.

In the morning Jack glowed, I'm going to take you home to mother.

They went to the bus depot and Jack paid for two tickets to Spartanburg, South Carolina.

You'll be my guest during my two week furlough.

Jack told his parents, He's my Army buddy.

The parents couldn't do enough for them. They shared a big bed in Jack's old room, where he'd lived as a boy. It had a very hot kerosene heater. Jack thought Padric was a bit too experienced for his taste, so they didn't have sex very often. That was the first real "home" Padric had ever seen. He could hardly believe it. One family in an entire house, just like Andy Hardy or Penrod where the sun streamed into the bedroom window in the morning, sparkling on the plaques and trophies Jack had won in school, the heater blasting out warm air.

At the end of two weeks Jack dropped him at the Spartanburg bus station, handing him enough fare for a ticket to Atlanta.

Padric strolled along Peachtree Street in Atlanta hoping that either Rhett or Ashley would catch his eye. He ate grits and gravy in a mom and pop café. He liked the salty, starchy, peppery, greasy taste. The food made his stomach feel full and content. He spent the night in a big hotel with a traveling salesman who was good to him.

In the morning the salesman drove him to the bus station, bought him a ticket instead of giving him cash.

He got off in Jacksonville, Florida and, right away, met a soldier who was fixated on a local homosexual murder.

The murderer hit his sugar daddy banker over the head with a plaster flamingo. It happened right here in Florida.

The soldier had lost his red, curly locks and was ashamed of it. He kept his hat on during sex.

The next day Padric walked through Jacksonville and on down to the highway to hitch a ride but kept walking and walked all the way to Manhattan Beach.

He picked up a fat old guy who was around forty years old, Reverend Robin Peabody of the Church of the Good Shepherd. The Reverend took him home to his pink Spanish-style house. He fed him peanut butter sandwiches and rum. Peanut butter and bread stuck to them, the Reverend took out his false teeth and dropped them in a glass filled with water and sucked him off under the covers. Padric guessed that the Reverend thought God couldn't see him.

The next day, the Reverend drove him to a restaurant near an old fort where Padric stuffed himself with shrimp Creole. The Reverend didn't eat, but lectured the whole while about sin.

After lunch the Reverend set him on the highway.

Goodbye, boy.

No rides picked him up, he got hungry and, by mid-afternoon, decided to walk to a roadside café and drink rum. The café was run by a blind man and his sighted wife. When he began feeling a little drunk, he went to the telephone and called the Reverend who drove up and got him, took him home and gave him another gum job. While the Reverend held an evening prayer service, Padric went to the movies. The Reverend was waiting when he got back, took him under the covers for another gumming.

The next day the Reverend gave him a little money, but played it safe and paid his bus fare.

He knew Miss Scarlet's address and got off the bus and asked instructions and walked the mile or so.

Miss Scarlet screamed when she saw him. He met Miss Scarlet's skinny working mother, lesbian sister, and pimple-faced fourteen-year-old brother. Miss Scarlet showed Padric their room. An old patchwork quilt decorated with scenes from the Civil War covered the bed.

You'll have to share a bed with me!

The other bed in the room was occupied by Miss Scarlet's repulsive brother who was a monster.

Two or three days later Miss Scarlet brought him to stay with another queen in town who drove a dry cleaning truck. Padric begged her, Oh show me how to drive!

The queen gave him a driving lesson. Later on, after a few drinks, Padric drove the dry cleaning truck off the highway, through a wire fence, and onto a field.

He shook his fist at the sky. With God as my witness, I'll never drive again!

That was the last time Padric McGarry ever drove, from that day to the end of his life.

President Roosevelt died in Warm Springs, Georgia ,two days after Padric's twentieth birthday. A dismal feeling went through him.

VE Day: Padric had missed the entire war except President Roosevelt's death a month before. Miss Scarlet yelled at him.

You're drinking too much. I hate it.

Miss Scarlet begged, Oh please stop drinking that filthy stuff.

Padric and Miss Scarlet had a fight.

Padric went to Delicate Frank's, a beachfront gay bar, and sat at the bar and drank rum and coke and whiskey sours. He wore a blue suit with a light blue oxford shirt. It was Halloween, 1945. The other queens at the bar— piss-elegant pink-tea queens—were all in costume. Padric wasn't in the mood. He just wanted to drink.

A policeman flashlight was shining into both his eyes. He opened them. He was lying in front of a crummy beachfront hotel. Beside him, neatly folded, his nice blue suit, his light blue Oxford shirt. He was naked. He felt a sharp, searing pain in his back, had what looked like a cigarette burn near his armpit. When he picked up his clothes there were charred holes, obviously from cigarette burns, through all of them.

The cop took Padric and his clothes and pack of Old Gold cigarettes to jail.

Prison record: 1) Drunk. 2) Suspected moral degenerate.

He was released. The cop gave him back his clothes and the Old Gold cigarettes.

The cop told—didn't suggest—Get out of town, boy!

His fifth arrest was a week later, in the next town. Padric wished he remembered more about it but all he saved was the official record, just "Vagrancy and drunk" so he guessed he wasn't doing anything degenerate. The record identified him as Patrick Jones. While still drunk he must have used the name of his mystery father—William Jones.

They gave him ten days for the vagrancy, five plus four or five for the drunkenness. That meant five dollars fine and four dollars court costs or five days in jail. He didn't have nine dollars but Miss Scarlet came and paid it so he could get out of jail after doing ten days.

Miss Scarlet took him to a little coffee joint next to the jail. Padric laughed off the arrest.

Miss Scarlet wasn't laughing.

If there's one thing I can't stand it's a drunken faggot. McGarry, you better go back north. Here's a bus ticket back to Jacksonville. One way!

He grabbed the ticket, turned his back on Miss Scarlet and swished out of the cafe.

He got a job as a counterman at a roadside truckers' joint called the Sleepy Bird Café. He was one of a dozen cooks and dishwashers and countermen. Most of the help lived in the boss's sister's rooming house next door to the café. Padric decided to go on the wagon. No booze. No sex. No Chesterfield smokes at night, only Old Golds in the day, all the crispy hash-browns he could eat. It couldn't hurt.

On his day off he stayed in the rooming house. He was lonely and restless, all the other roomers were at work. Methodically he went from room to room and searched everyone's closets. He appropriated a pale pink mohair sweater. Up in the attic he noticed three lovely tan matching suitcases. The next week, on his day off, he went up to the attic and took the suitcases and carried them over to the local hock shop—Uncle Sam's Loans.

Uncle Sam looked at the suitcases.

Ten dollars.

Each?

For the lot.

Padric took the ten and went over to a bar owned by two gay guys. He drank and enjoyed himself.

Later he bought a bottle of cheap whiskey and went to the local movie theater. He bought a ticket and sat alone in the balcony of the theater, uncapping the bottle, sipped. A few rows below were two young sailors. Padric felt old and worn out compared to the crisp young ones. He addressed a comment to the sailors. One got up and walked across the aisle and went to sleep. The other walked back two rows, sat next to him. Immediately they had their hands in each other's pants.

He woke. The theater porter was shaking him. The bottle was empty. So was the theater.

He walked outside. The sunlight hit him. He remembered the Reverend. In his wallet, no money, but a bus ticket to Jacksonville.

He sat at the counter of the restaurant at the bus depot and counted his change. He had seven cents. He ordered a five cent cup of coffee. A guy he knew from the rooming house was having a cup of coffee too.

How come you're not at work at the Sleepy Bird?

I've quit. I'm going to Jacksonville. I got a friend there.

Good luck.

The bus ground its gears, pulled onto the road.

Half way to Jacksonville, during a rest stop, two southern cops—wearing cowboy hats and boots—clambered on. They stood in the aisle with drawn guns staring down at the seated passengers one at a time. They walked right up to him.

Name?

William Jones.

They knew he was shucking.

Stand up, boy.

One stuck a cold gun into his back.

Walk slow and easy.

It was a one-cell jailhouse. Sitting in the cell he could hear the cop on the telephone.

...we've got that thar Yankee you fellas was looking for.

He dozed in the cell until about three in the morning when two detectives came for him.

They handcuffed him and put him in the back seat of their car. They began to drive. A heavy fog rolled in from the ocean. The driver couldn't see a thing. The car crawled along. One of the detectives got out of the car and led the way through the thick fog.

While awaiting trial, he was put into the county jail where he caught impetigo right away, had little pitted sores from his ankles to his waist as well as erupting pustules that itched something awful. The sores became brown crusts after they'd been viciously scratched. Although he complained, no one took him to a doctor. A lesbian in the Women's Tank heard his lament and passed some sulfa ointment to him through the bars as she was leaving for court. He picked off the crusts one by one.

He was tried and felt very old. He pleaded guilty and was sentenced, had made the Big Leagues since those three suitcases were worth more than a hundred dollars—grand larceny. The sentence was three years of hard labor in the state penitentiary.

It was 1946, three months before his twenty-first birthday.

The warden had a big office with a big desk. His name was H.J. Bush. He was big and seemed like a real southern plantation gentleman right out of *Gone With The Wind* like Scarlet O'Hara's father before the war except that he had lanky white hair and a thin, mealy mouth.

Sit down.

He sat.

Yeuah Yankees come down heah to the fair south and attempt to rape and rob, and thank you can get away fro it. But while youah heah we're goin' make sure you understand you just can't do that, Yankee Boy. You gonna work. You were sentenced to three yeahs hahd labuh. You understand that?

Bush gave him a copy of the Official Rule Book. It contained precise rules on when to get up, how to talk to the hacks, what the privileges were. The unofficial rules, which he quickly learned, were just as important, maybe even more so. For instance, there was nothing in the fair south rule book about earning money from other inmates. Money was everything in that prison. The inmates were allowed to have it, and he discovered that as a twenty-one-year-old new fish—who was referred to as "gal-boy"—he was valuable merchandise and could earn a lot with his Irish tail and his Yankee head. Quickly he realized he would be needing a lot of money to avoid constantly eating fatback, grits with gravy and collard greens. Canned goods from the commissary were expensive. He guessed somebody was making a dollar off the cons.

Padric's four "old men" in Central:

Danny-the-Dentist. Danny had been a dentist outside. In prison he was an inmate assistant to the prison dentist. They met when Padric went to get a tooth pulled.

Danny told him, Most convicts let their teeth fall out rather than visit us, are afraid of anesthesia, afraid of what they'll say when out cold. Aren't you afraid?

No. I like anesthesia.

Danny was ugly, had pockmarks, but a strong face. They had frantic sex in Danny's little storeroom off the dental office. Afterwards Danny painted his gums for gingivitis.

The Violent One had lots of cash. He'd been in a psychiatric hospital for years, had had electrotherapy, hydrotherapy, been put in big tubs, withstood freezing cold baths, been hosed with hot and also cold water.

I had a hemorrhoidectomy years ago for free.

The Violent One worked at the hospital. He brought Padric A.K. from the hospital where he worked. A.K. was alcohol used to wash surgical instruments. It tasted awful even if it was mixed with fruit juice. The Violent One would cry like a new baby after orgasm. He couldn't stand to be around Padric after that, would run away the moment his fly was zipped back up.

The third was called The Goat because he looked like one. He really made good love. The Goat had an allergy to milk, every time he drank any his face broke out in a rash.

The fourth "old man" was Three Fingered Joe. He had been a newspaper man who had salt and pepper hair. As an outside Trusty, he could leave prison and bring back "things." He brought Padric pints of White Lightning. He called him "Mah Pussy." Every time he said "Mah Pussy" Padric had to laugh. When Padric first arrived, he was put in with the general population. For a while he shared a cell with Miss Teddy Morris whose real name was Roosevelt Morris, a thirty-year-old hulk of raw-boned effeminacy.

Whenever he talked about that prison later in his life he called it the Southern Chain Gang instead of Central Prison, because chain gang was what it really was. Like the man said—"hahd labuh." Prisoners didn't actually wear chains nor did they wear striped suits any more like *Cool Hand Luke* but if they thought someone might try to escape—having "rabbit in the blood"– he was made to wear leg irons night and day.

Every day Padric went out to work on a road gang on the state highways, into a road camp. Road camps were scattered all over the area. He'd work out of a particular camp for several days running. He learned about a pick-axe, a grubbing hoe that broke up the ground, a yo-yo that cut grass and had a long wooden handle, a steel arch with a razor-sharp blade. The blade of the yo-yo blistered his hands.

A local guy told him, Piss on your blisters. It toughens up your skin.

That same guy confided, I ain't had sex in eleven years.

Padric pissed on his hands but it didn't help. His hands hurt like hell at night.

He learned to do tricks with the yo-yo axe. He could do twirls like a cheerleader, he could swing it around his body in a circle, changing hands, cutting grass all the way around in a circle.

The men worked in a line while out on the road. One day a guy begged him, Cut the heel of my leg with your yo-yo.

If a man's Achilles tendon got cut accidentally he could get off work. Padric got nauseous at the idea, he couldn't do it but another guy did.

Usually the men worked for the state but occasionally they were rented to a private contractor for a dollar an hour. On one job he was told to work on a cesspool with Miss Jew Baby, a queen from New York. He and Miss Jew Baby were the known gal-boys on that road gang. The job was to clean the foundation of a house that included the cesspool. That is, the "men" cleaned the foundation, and Miss Jew Baby and Padric were to clean the shit even though Padric didn't know what a cesspool was.

Miss Jew Baby shrieked, I'm a lady. I'm not going in any cesspool!

The shotgun guard beat on her shoulder with his axe-handle a couple of time until Miss Jew Baby begged, Oh God stop. I'll do it.

Miss Jew Baby put a handkerchief around her face.

The shotgun guard told her, Take that off, stop acting uppity.

So Padric and Miss Jew Baby got down into the cesspool and filled buckets with shitty water.

The guard sing-songed at them, Gaze upon a white alligator, y'all have good fortune in the coming year! Three lucky cons discovered a nest of eighteen male baby blue-eyed, white-skinned 'gators in our swamp. Maybe you'll have good luck too…

The guard thought he was very funny but it scared the Yankees shitless.

It took hours but they cleaned out the entire ten by twenty cesspit. Once finished there was nowhere to wash, leaving Padric and Miss Jew Baby stinking to high heaven for the rest of the day and no one came near.

One night he was in bed in his skivvy shorts. Although it was a double-bunker cell there was nobody in the upper. He heard footsteps coming down the row of cells, heard them stop at his cell, heard a voice whisper, I'm gonna fuck you, boy.

He knew the voice. It was Thomas T. Thomas from Tennessee, called T.T., a turnkey on his floor. T.T. was six-four, good looking in a mountain kind of way, a long, lean, lanky mountain man. The deadlock must have been left open, which meant that T.T. could get into the cells with his own key. The key clicked in the keyhole, he walked in.

I'm gonna fuck you, boy.

No you're not.

Yes I am, you better get ready.

T.T. got undressed, he ripped off Padric's skivvy shorts. He pulled out a big jar of Vaseline, scooped out a handful, jammed some of it up inside and whammo. He must have knocked over the jar because it broke, but by then they were past paying attention. For the rest of his life Padric remembered T.T. as the best sex he ever had in prison. T.T. fucked him so good, he came, and more than once too. And all night.

The next day T.T. strode up to him in the prison yard. When he saw that no one was around he stuck out his hand and pumped Padric's up and down.

Sorry I didn't kiss you last night, McGarry. I had a cold and I didn't want to give it to you. But I really want to thank you for the good loving you gave me, you broke the goddamned cold completely.

He and Miss Jew Baby were constantly harassed. A Yankee gal-boy on a southern chain gang is like being black, cross-eyed, hunchbacked and a drunk, all at once. A Jewish gal-boy was even worse. Out on the road, Miss Jew Baby suddenly ran down the highway flapping her arms.

I'm a tweet-tweet bird.

The guard trained his gun on Miss Jew Baby but didn't fire it. Later they took Miss Jew Baby away to the hospital.

Alongside the highway, the crew began digging a passage for a culvert through a swampy mess of water moccasins, insects and smelly plants. Padric was given a number eight shovel for digging and, like all the other men, wore "monkey shoes," which were high boots made of soft skin. When he got past the asphalt, he encountered brown muck that stuck to his shovel like molasses. The trick was to twist the shovel, to make the sticky muck drop off.

They'd been digging for several hours. The gang was standing in a trench. Padric was struggling to twist the muck off his shovel. An old Captain was watching him real close.

Put some mud on that shovel gal-boy, gimme some mud or gimme your ass.

Padric sang out, Yassuh Captain, you get the mud Captain.

A few more shovelfuls and the Captain shouted at him again.

Put some mud on that shovel gal-boy, gimme some mud or gimme your ass.

But the Captain didn't like something.

Goddamit gal-boy, you ain't doin't nothing and you holding up my boys. Now stand up here, and when the boys throw the mud up, you put it thar, yonder and cheer.

Yassuh boss, yassuh Captain.

He thought, Love to kiss you ass, boss.

He started to make two piles of brown muck as the other inmates threw it up out of the trench. One was at one end of the trench—yonder—the other at the other end—thar. But, where was cheer? After half an hour the Captain walked over, screaming.

Gal-boy I told you to put that stuff thar...

He pointed to the pile at Padric's feet "...yonder," pointing to the other end of the trench "...and cheer" pointing, as far as Padric could tell, exactly where he'd pointed for yonder.

Yassuh.

He went on with the same two piles. He was afraid to tell the Captain that he didn't understand him.

The Captain came over and yelled some more, but Padric still couldn't dope out what he meant.

The Captain added, ...if I have to come and tell you one more time, gal-boy, I'll beat the shit out of you.

The Captain took off for lunch. The two piles got larger and larger. Late in the afternoon the Captain returned.

Goddammit, I warned you, gal-boy, and now you're going to get it, you Yankee sonofabitch.

The Captain was sweating heavily, and rushed at him. Padric dropped the shovel and threw up his arms to ward him off. Captain, I don't know what you mean by 'cheer'…

You callin' me stupid, boy? You callin' me ignorant?

The Captain swung at his head and shoulders with a lighter knot which was an axe-handle without the metal axe head that all guards wore stuck through their belts. The Captain swung it like a policeman's Billy club.

Padric ran, screamed. The Captain ran after him, beating him with every shriek, chased him into and out of the trench they were digging for the culvert, into and out of the swampy grass, up along the side of the road. There were shotgun guards along the road. Whenever he ran toward one of them, the guard would snarl, his lip curling.

Get your ass out of here or I'll blow it off.

The Captain was exhausted. He stopped and walked away. Padric was bruised, shaking, bleeding in the middle of the road. He screamed his lungs raw.

As he stood like a lone statue screaming, a dozen or so men on the gang walked over and surrounded him like wild animals do when they have a sick animal in their midst. He was in the center. The others faced outward and away. He began to cry right from the pit of his belly, in the middle of the hot southern road.

The workday was finished, the prisoners were slowly loaded aboard a truck.

Padric whispered to one of the men he knew, They're going to put me in the Box for trying to run away. I'm sure.

The Box was outside the barbed wire fence that surrounded the camp. It was a tin room made of planks the size of three men lying down. Inside they'd leave a pail of water and a second empty pail. When a prisoner was sentenced to the Box for punishment, his clothes were removed. He was usually sentenced to the Box for three days without any food, just a pint bottle of castor oil. He was given a white cotton hospital gown. Inside, one or two prisoners would lie in the dark, with very little light, very little air trickling between the planks. The sun burned into the tin roof. They would sip the water. They had been ordered to drink the castor oil that made them shit horribly. The guards thought this awful shitting was very funny. It was a sport—two prisoners fighting to shit in a shit-filled bucket.

But he wasn't put in the Box. Instead, he was marched through the gates with the other prisoners. He was frisked, and sent, along with everyone else, to the wooden Army-style barracks that served as bunks. Two inmates took care of him. They helped him undress and put him under a shower. A couple of men came into the shower with him and sponged each swollen place.

He was exhausted, climbed onto his bunk and slept through supper. (While in the road camp, it was not against the rules to miss supper, also the convicts could move freely within the camp.) He went into a deep sleep.

He woke in the night. Being summer, it was still light out. His hands were bruised and even more swollen, everything throbbed. He felt very calm, very logical. He knew what to do, and how to do it and dragged his aching body into the recreation area to find John the Water Boy.

He whispered into John's ear, I'll have sex with you tonight if you'll bring me a straight-edge razor blade.

Okay. I'll send the inmate floor-walker to your barracks later tonight.

Padric went back to his bunk and slept again.

About 2:30 a.m. after the shotgun guard outside the barracks had gone to sleep, the floor-walker—a mountain of a man like T.T.—woke him. They tip-toed through the halls.

John the Water Boy had hung blankets around his bunk. Padric crawled inside.

First give it to me, Padric insisted.

The floor-walker escorted him back to his bunk. He owned two silk scarves, he often held them in his hand at night. One was small with red and green stripes, the other large, Chinese red. He knotted the smaller, multi-colored, striped kerchief around his left arm, just above the elbow. Then, he tied the big blood-red one around his neck like a cape. It hung down loosely over his shoulders and chest so all that could be seen was his head sticking out of a red silk tent. The olive-drab blanket on his cot covered up the rest of him.

After pumping up the vein by clenching and unclenching his fist a few times, he took the shiny new blade and traced a straight line across the inside of his left elbow. Pain and a trickle of blood seeped out. Not much blood. He hated blood. He was chickenshit. He held his breath for a few minutes, reconsidered, then, he lay back. He felt the pain of the beating and he knew everything would just go on and on, day after day after day, and he really didn't want to face it. Without looking, he dug deep down in the same place, as far as he could go into his flesh. That's when it really hurt but he was afraid it still wasn't enough so he made a second gash about half an inch below the first one on his inner arm. Next he cut crosswise a few times, joining the two slashes. He could feel blood gushing out, felt a rhythmic pulse. He lay with his eyes closed and his bleeding arm under the covers, pumping his fist, with his knees drawn up against his belly so anyone who passed and looked at him would think he was asleep under the covers.

Blood flowed. He felt it fill up that sway-backed hollow place that all cheap cots have when you lie on them.

It began to go dark inside his eyelids but he must have been moving around without realizing because the next thing he knew there was a lot of noise and the lights went on. It seems the blanket had come off and the floor-walker had seen blood with the light from his flashlight. The floor-walker made all the other inmates stand up alongside their bunks while he notified the guard in the cage who called the Captain. An inmate took his multi-colored tourniquet and a spoon and tightened it up so much that Padric's arm swelled up three times its normal size.

He felt nothing, was going on and off like a blinking light.

The only one they could get to come to the prison in the night was a country veterinarian who looked like Li'l Abner. The vet was mad as hell for being awakened at such an ungodly hour.

You pull me out of sleep to help some Yankee? Too bad he didn't cut his balls off.

The vet used a fat, curved needle and stitched his arm. He bandaged the cuts.

Get plenty of rest, boy, drink lots of orange juice, hehe.

The vet made a few mores dirty southern hehe's and walked away. The thin mattress was drenched with blood. A few of the men lifted the soaked mattress and leaned it against the wall. They covered the bedsprings with blankets.

Padric lay on the bedsprings. He heard the camp wake up, dress, march to breakfast. Someone brought him a tray with a plate loaded down with gravy soaked biscuits.

In the afternoon they helped him into a station wagon and drove him back to the Central Prison where he was put into the hospital.

After about ten days the doctor was leaving for a trip. He looked at the raw wound.

Boot him out of here, the doctor told the nurse.

To punish him for his act and to scare him into not doing it again, he was put on Bread Row. Bread Row was a jail within the jail. He was put into a cell made out of rocks that were wet day and night. All he got fed was little biscuits in the shape of cat-heads.

Every day H.J. Bush, the superintendent, visited him in his dingy cell.

Gal-boy, you got your mind right?

No sir, Captain.

Everyday, for fourteen days, Bush visited him and asked him the same question.

Gal-boy, you got your mind right?

On day fourteen H.J. Bush came by.

He told the guard, Take this goddam gal-boy out of here. He's crazy.

He spent time in the Dark Cell.

Eventually he was moved to White "Forgotten Row." Since the prison was segregated, there was a Black "Forgotten Row" and a White "Forgotten Row." (Only the Homo Block was integrated—black girls, white girls, you name it.) Across the inner courtyard on White Death Row he could see Billy Scott who was waiting to be executed. While drunk Billy had raped a married lady in her back yard where she had been hanging up wet clothes on a clothesline. To keep her from hollering, he choked her to death and they caught him and he was sentenced to death in the electric chair.

Padric imagined that Billy was a gentle person now. Billy was young, blond, had a terrific body.

Billy Scott sent Marvin the Turnkey to Padric with a love note. The next day Padric sent a note back. Notes went back and forth. Billy had learned to write in the death house, had been illiterate before.

Feeling lonely, during the night, Padric yelled at the top of his voice.

Billy!

Billy woke up and yelled back.

Pat!

Billy and Padric yelled back and forth to each other.

The commotion could be heard all over Forgotten Row and Death Row. In the office, the hack put down his work.

He yelled into the bullhorn, Who's making that goddam racket?

I am.

Oh you like it over there on Death Row, gal-boy?

Billy's there, he thought.

I sure do, Captain.

Well, we'll sure fix you ass.

The next day he was transferred to Death Row. Not White Death Row, but Black Death Row, around the corner from Billy.

The southern blacks started singing. The lights dimmed and turned green.

Marvin the Turnkey told him, We had an execution last night.

Marvin the Turnkey was six foot two, had skinny arms tattooed with butcher knives dripping teardrop-shaped drops of blood. He truly loved Padric. One night he came to his cell and had sex. Marvin the Turnkey ran the tattoo parlor. He carved freehand with a tattoo gun that had been crafted from a toothbrush melted around a sewing needle. Marvin used blue-green ink, the color used in the printing shop.

Want a tattoo?

No Marvin.

I'll give you one for nothin.

No. I'm afraid of needles.

In all the weeks of yelling back and forth he and Billy had never touched or seen each other up close. Padric knew when Billy was taken for a shower. He talked the old trusty, Whitey, into letting him out of the cell at the same time.

I must have a shower.

Billy left his slippers toe to toe along the wall. Billy and Padric were finally alone in the shower room. They lay down on the floor of the shower, began touching.

The electric chair is next door, through the steel door, Billy told him.

Padric didn't want to hear but Billy spoke into his ear.

I can hear the hum of its motor and also the drills and saws they use when they do the autopsy right after the burning?

Billy couldn't keep his hard on. Padric tried everything he knew to bring it back but nothing happened so they lay on the floor of the shower until Whitey came back in. Whitey opened the door where the electric chair was. Billy and Padric looked at it.

Whitey was chewing a wad of tobacco. He spit into his hand.

Thomas Edison invented it but George Westinghouse added alternating current transformers to make the wires hot enough to kill you. It's man-made lightening, fellas.

Billy hollered like hell when he was being taken to the electric chair. Padric pressed his hands against his ears. He heard the black men sing three times during the night. Once for Billy, and he didn't know why else. The lights dimmed and went green.

For months after that night he imagined an electrode being applied to the sexy calf of Billy's right leg, another electrode being attached to the crown of his handsome head, also straps pinning down his arms, legs, chest. At night he dreamed that Billy's body was leaping against the leather straps while a wisp of gray smoke seeped from under the electrodes and Billy's hands went bright red then white, the cords of his neck standing out like strong steel bands.

He spent eight months on Black Death Row.

He received a letter from Mary.

Dear Padric, Please do not come back home when you get out this time. Go somewhere else and try to make a life for yourself. You've caused me and your two half-sisters enough trouble. We want to live our lives in peace. Mary

He wrote back:

I, Padric McGarry, am disowning you people. I will go out and have a life of my own like you say, and that's it.

He began to cry. Marvin heard him and came into his cell.

What's happened?

I disowned my mother.

Marvin put his arms around him. He cried all the more then because the least little bit of tenderness made him melt. When Marvin left, he sat down on his bunk, wiped away the tears with the back of his hand.

They took him from Death Row to work in the gristmill. Gristmill was for the sick, the lame and the lazy, and also for people like Padric who were coming off punishment. It had a great waterwheel that was made to turn by rapid running water. It was very noisy when corn was poured into the hopper and the large furrowed upper stone began turning against the fixed furrowed netherstone, as meal flowed down from a wooden spout making ground corn.

Padric's face and clothes became dusty white in the gristmill.

On gristmill, he stripped tobacco, shucked corn and cut up vegetables. A queen showed him how to catch water moccasin snakes in the stream that flowed through the prison. He clasped a moccasin right away but it slipped out of his hand. The queen caught one and twirled it in the air, snapped its head off.

That's how you kill it.

He caught another, twirled it through the air, the head snapped off.

Padric and the queen on gristmill skinned snakes and made belts with the snakeskin. They sold the belts.

From stripping tobacco, his hands got raw, were criss-crossed with cuts as if somebody had taken a razor blade and made little doodles on his palms.

After two weeks on gristmill he was released. He'd done thirty-four and a half months at hard labor for grand larceny. The queens from gristmill baked two sweet potato pies for him as a farewell gift. He was twenty-three, had fifty dollars, was a free man.

Padric drank up twenty-five of the fifty dollars he had at the first bar he saw. When he counted the money he had left he didn't have enough for a bus ticket to meet Miss Teddy Morris in Indiana. He decided to hitch-hike. The plan had been to join her in Indiana and rob the town blind. Miss Morris knew how to get in all the stores and needed a smart, fast helper – a clever "girl" from the Bronx.

A truck driver picked him up where he stood at the side of the road.

Padric begged, Get me the hell out of the fair south as fast as you can.

They drove for a few hours.

The truck driver said, I'm staying overnight in Savannah with my girlfriend. If you want, I'll meet you in the morning.

I'll be here.

He left the brown cardboard suitcase in the parked truck and wandered around Savannah, finding a place to sleep that was run by Brothers. He found a pay telephone and called Mary collect.

Don't worry, I won't come home.

Good.

Could you send me some money. I'm broke.

I'll try to borrow twenty-five dollars from your Uncle John O'Malley.

The Brothers served breakfast. He met a big, young, masculine Polish guy as he stuffed himself with toast and oatmeal.

I'll show you how to find the telegraph office, he offered.

Twenty-five dollars was waiting for him there. The Polish guy was so nice Padric gave him half the twenty-five because he was just as broke. That's when he realized he didn't have the slightest idea where to find his truck driver, his truck or his suitcase.

What the hell.

The Polish guy took him to the bus station. He had enough for a ticket to the Indiana town named Bloomington. When he was about to get on the bus, the Polish guy got a huge erection.

Don't leave me Pat. Stay with me.

But he got on the bus.

Twelve days after the discharge from Central Prison, he was in an Indiana County Jail.

Charge: Vagrancy. Sentence: Thirty days.

Across from the jail was a firehouse. Through the small window in his cell he could see the firehouse, could watch the firemen to-ing and fro-ing. Christmas was coming. He serenaded the firemen through the window:

> *"Oh come all ye faithful,*
> *Joyful and triumph-ant.*
> *Oh come ye, oh co-ome ye*
> *To Be-eth-le-hem*
> *Come and ah-dore him,*
> *Born the kind of a-ang-els"*

About to be released, he telephoned Mary. Collect. Mary wasn't home but he got his young half-sister Elizabeth on the telephone.

I need money so I can spring myself from jail.

I'll send you my Christmas money.

I'll give it back to you when I get back to New York.

You're coming back to New York?
Yes.
When?
Soon.

He went by bus to Chicago.

He discovered the North Clark Street bars.

He lived with a pair of lesbians.

He was gang-raped by an Italian "social club."

He had a drunken incident in Oshkosh, Wisconsin, the place where they manufactured doors, windows, blinds, matches, where there were saw mills and rivers for logging.

He returned to Chicago, stayed a year. His landlady taught him how to plant bulbs in shallow bowls and then to keep them in the coolness of his dark closet. He'd put a two-by-four over the radiator and set the bowls on the board. Crocus, paper white narcissus, snowdrops appeared from, it seemed, nowhere. There was a café around the corner that served cheap "Broasted Chicken—All You Can Eat." Also fries dipped in spitting fat.

Padric said it was the happiest year he'd known but couldn't explain why.

1949, December. He crossed the brown, wide Mississippi with high levees by freight train. He arrived in New Orleans to look up at the iron balconies and red walls. He heard music coming out of every door, stepped through the first one. Drink up, the gent offering a rum punch told him. Quickly he was drunk, crashed onto a dark patio, out like a light among palms and vines.

He came to. A dog was humping his foot. His fear of dogs tightened his gut. He smelled strong gardenia, scented rose, butterfly lily. The dog growled. He got up, leaned on a banana tree and pushed at the dog with his shoe. When the dog backed away, Padric stumbled back into the street. He stumbled around a park and then slept under a live oak. When he woke, he was hidden under a dense hanging beard of Spanish moss that was full of jabbering, fat cardinals. The dog that had adopted him had turned into a cat. He threw up—gallons of lumpy, spicy food mixed with strong booze—into the bushes.

He fell for a shrimp fisherman who lisped through missing teeth. The fisherman had boils on his neck, told him, after sex against a wall, I'm due at the fleet. Wait back on Canal Street.

New Year's Eve 1950, not twenty minutes after midnight, Padric hit on a bartender in a gay bar. No-Chin Virginia was kind to him and let him stay in her funky house hidden behind rust bougainvillea and a drooping, insect-infested coral-flower called cry baby tree, a fifteen minute walk from Canal.

Humid spring weather closed around him. No-Chin Virginia stirred up mint juleps. Quickly insects covered Padric's pink arms and face with itching bites. As he scratched, No-Chin Virginia stirred the pitcher.

They don't eat me, you must taste good.

He hitch-hiked west. Between rides he walked along the highways until he reached Houston, a sprawling city, abandoned houses on the outskirts.

A new friend: Miss Green droned on and on about her idol, Sam Houston, Houston named for General Sam Houston, "The Raven" who was shot with a cannon. His horse fell. He mounted another. It fell too. Though his ankle was shattered, the General remounted a third horse and charged. He didn't know he was in pain. In eighteen minutes the Mexicans were routed. Six hundred fifty Mexicans died. Seven Texans died, no shit.

Miss Green had acne pustules across her shoulder blades.

Don't drink like that Paddy, you're no chicken anymore, you need your wits about you much more.

Speak for yourself.

And how. And how. Like now when I'm off the roof.

He and Miss Green took a freight train to Los Angeles. They jumped before the train entered Union Station, and crossed the tracks until they found a way into Union

Station. It looked like a Spanish mission or a Moorish palace. Padric had seen Carole Lombard, Barbara Stanwick, Groucho Marx, and Cary Grant walk in or out of its cool interior.

Miss Green pointed out City Hall.

They walked down Los Angeles Street.

Miss Green told him, This here's the garment district. There's always day work for jobbers. Care for a job?

Let's discuss it over a drink.

They walked down Los Angeles Street until it became skid row.

Cecil B. DeMille, where are you when I need you?

Miss Green changed into white Capri pants and turned a trick. They drank wine, got tipsy, took a taxi to the Hollywood Walk of Fame, found a bar there.

Padric ordered, One pink lady.

Miss Green swung her pear-shaped hips around.

Meet me on the Walk of Fame, or better yet, at Fredericks. You'll find me buyin' trashy lingerie.

Padric didn't see Miss Green for a week. He met her by chance at a gay bar.

He spent two nights with a John who wore white ducks and a blue blazer that had a missing gold button. He got beaten up by a cop who hated gay people.

He and Miss Green took menial jobs with the Clyde Beatty Circus. The colored poster showed the lion tamer holding the jaw of a lion wide open with his bare hands while a beautiful woman with flaming red hair stuck her head into the lion's mouth. The lion's teeth gleamed. Pad-

ric thought he looked like that beautiful woman but without red-tinged hair. Maybe one day he would dye his hair
flaming red.

He became "The Cat Queen." All men in the circus
had nicknames: Camel Man, Big Humpy, Little Humpy,
Big Nose, Peanut Nose Bob, Whitey, Shorty, Frenchy,
Rattlesnake Red.

He got friendly with Pat the Elephant Man who pushed
wagons in the mud, unloaded the trains, unrolled canvas,
raised the poles as the elephant pulled and Pat prodded
the elephant's flat, narrow head. When the elephant refused to cross a shaky bridge, Pat took him down to the
waters edge and the elephant swam across. On muddy
days, the elephant had canvas shoes put on his tender feet
so they wouldn't get sore.

Leaving Miss Green asleep, not leaving a note, Padric
and Pat the Elephant Man left the circus and hitch-hiked
toward New York.

They split up on the road.

He arrived back in New York, June 1950. Alone. Summer was sticky and humid. A dog's summer. He immediately went to the old places. He needed a big drink.

A winter afternoon. He turned a trick in Brooklyn
apartment at the intersection of Flatbush Avenue, Nevins
and Fulton Streets. The trick bleat like a sick sheep then
passed out. Padric stole his money, a bottle of gin and a

bottle of red wine from a shelf. He put each bottle into a coat pocket and tip-toed out onto the back porch on the second floor. He gazed at the neighborhood, sat on the railing, lit a cigarette.

He was looped out of his mind and was wondering what to do next. Then suddenly he was not sitting there anymore, but was down on the ground lying in the snow on his back, breath knocked out of him and moaning like a wounded seal. He lay there a good ten minutes until somebody helped him up and walked him to the subway. The first thing he checked were the two bottles. Miraculously they had survived the fall. That's when he took it into his "fruit head"—as he always called it—to ride the subway way the hell out to the end of the line in Queens and see Mary. He hadn't laid eyes on her since he'd run away from home a good six years earlier.

He did that and got off the IRT subway in Flushing. He took a bus outside May's Department Store and another that traveled along blocks of brick apartment buildings and frame houses, stores, YMCAs, schools, empty lots. He walked for many blocks past red brick attached houses each with trees and real lawns. He nipped away at his bottles, slugging on the gin for warmth and chased it with wine to kill the taste. An hour later, he couldn't walk any more because his back was hurting where he'd fallen on it. It began to snow. It was heavy snow.

He was still drunk, was half walking, half crawling. The police drove by, stopped him. He showed a letter from his sister. They put him in the police car.

The cops dumped him out on Mary's doorstep. The snow suddenly was raging. His back hurt like hell.

Mary opened the door. The only thing he noticed was that her eyebrows needed plucking. She took him in, told him to wipe the snow off his clothes, put him to bed.

The house had five rooms. Jeanne was living with Mary and Mary's new man, a little Dutchman. Another baby had been given up for adoption to some cousins.

Every day Mary brought him some food.

Every day she told him, You should leave as soon as possible because I want to keep this guy, I don't want him to get irritated by you and your ways. But didn't throw him out.

Two weeks passed. He began to feel better, to walk around the house. Mary made a pile of baloney and mayonnaise sandwiches on soft Dugan's bread. She ate one too, between bites he plucked her eyebrows, wiping each hair from the tweezers onto a napkin. It was like old times, he made Mary laugh, he made her eyes fill with tears when he yanked a hair with a deep root.

Mary asked him to fill her big bucket with Westpine and water and mop across the kitchen and bathroom floor. When the floor was spotless, Mary brought him his clothes, washed and folded neatly.

Get dressed.

He got dressed.

Mary fed him homemade wine in a jelly glass. You gotta go.

She gave him two boxes of food and took him by the arm, walked him to the bus.

This bus will take you to the train, the train will take you to the city.

Patric climbed onto the bus. He never saw her again.

July 1950. Sentence: Eight months. Charge: Petty larceny committed in a YMCA. Arrest: Number Eight.

Back on the Homo Block. He was too old to be a "new" face.

Released March 1951.

He used the name Carol Jones, appropriating the last name of the father listed on the bastard birth certificate.

He became friends with Miss Corky, and began to hang out at Greenwich Village bars. If desperate, he slept on a bench in Washington Square Park, the bench closest to the bronze statue of Garibaldi or else close to the Arch at the foot of Fifth Avenue beside the two statues of George Washington, one in uniform, one in civilian dress, both on tall bases.

He made a pass at a Marine. Just when he'd slipped onto his knees, he felt a fist crashing against his scalp. The Marine beat him up, cracked his shoulder blade. He crawled to a bar. Miss Corky, a couple of lesbians and homos helped him to St. Vincent's Emergency Room.

Invited to a nice cocktail party in a nice apartment off Fifth Avenue, Padric rifled purses and coat pockets in the bedroom while the guests were in the living room and the lights of the city blurred.

He slept on the BMT subway.

He slept in other village parks, or at the river.

He slept in Pennsylvania Station.

He took a "Sentimental Journey" back to his childhood neighborhood in the Bronx where he tried to break into an apartment in Joey Rust's old building.

He was arrested.

Charge: Unlawful entry. Ninth Arrest.

Back in the Homo Block he met Timmins. Timmins was a guard. Timmins wrote love letters to him:

I'll set you up in a furnished room. What do you say?

Padric wrote back:

Give me the money. I'll find a room. Then I'll let you know where I am.

Timmons gave him an envelope filled with money the night before his release.

He was released.

He gave Timmons the slip.

At a party, he burgled a sleeping guest's pockets. He slugged down a bottle of wine on the fire escape of a cheap hotel on Lexington Avenue. Passed out.

He was arrested.

Tenth arrest.

He and a rock-hard Italian guy were chained together and taken by a lone guard on a train along the Hudson River. The stop was Ossining, New York. Sing Sing.

After getting off the train they crossed Hunter Street, passed people who didn't blink at the sight of two men in handcuffs, and reached the armored gate. Sing Sing was built of gray stone under a high bluff. A streaked sunset of yellows and reds blushed behind the bluff where, someone said, the Sinck Indians had once built signal fires.

Inside, he heard a whistle blow.

All in. All in.

Sing Sing had a knit shop, a dye shop, a shoe shop, a mattress shop, a brush shop a sheet-metal shop. The tiers of cells rose six high and were set back to back. The front of the cells had galleries that were about ten feet from the wall and encircled the prison. No sunlight ever reached the interior of any cell, nor was there much ventilation.

The job assigned was to work in the Sing Sing mail-room.

He started a love affair with the prison electrician.

He had a new friend named Harry who'd stolen Gladys Swarthout's jewelry.

Harry asked, Where you from Paddy?

The Bronx. New York.

Christine Jorgensen grew up in the Bronx. Lucky you.

Harry was an expert on Christine Jorgensen, showed headlines from the *Daily News*: *Bronx Youth is Happy Woman After Medication, 6 Operations.*

And *Ex-GI Becomes Blonde Beauty!*

How?

Harry gave him a pile of clippings from Hearst's *American Weekly* in which were Christine's own words to her parents in the Bronx: *At times it is obvious that something has gone wrong. We humans are perhaps the greatest chemical reactions in the world. Among the greatest working parts of our bodies are the glands. An imbalance in the glandular system puts the body under a strain in an effort to adjust...I am the same old Brud, my dears, but nature made the mistake I have had corrected. And now I am your daughter!*

And she looks like Tallulah Bankhead, Harry pointed at a photo.

Padric studied the photo of a blond woman in a mink coat. She did look like Tallulah. To think she grew up right on Dudley Avenue in the Bronx. Christine was appearing at the Latin Quarter doing comedy, singing "Getting to Know You" from *The King and I.*

He remained in Sing Sing for three months. January—March 1953 awaiting news, couldn't get "Getting to Know You" out of his head for most of it.

Conviction: Grand larceny.

Sentence: Two-and-a-half- to five years in state prison.

The morning of his twenty-eighth birthday, April 10, 1953, he was put in chains and waited in his cell at Sing Sing until he was taken by an officer to a station wagon and driven to the train station. From the window of the station wagon, he saw thick trunked trees. At first he saw only blackened bark, then—looking more closely—he saw pale, speckled pepper-moths in clusters.

The officer accompanied him on the train upstate to Clinton State Prison in Dannemora, New York, in the Adirondack Mountains.

He was put into general population at Dannemora for the first few days.

An old lifer told him, Get your denture plate while you're inside and it's free.

Nick, an Italian, serving twenty years for murder, didn't like Padric sharing his cell. Nick hung around with what he called the "elite" who in his book were the Italians. He told Padric why he didn't like him.

You can't be a rat here, and you can't be a rapist, you can't be a child molester to hang around with us, and you especially can't be a rapist or a queer.

Nick had pin-ups on this wall. He had gross girlie magazines hidden under his mattress, also dusty webs made by spiders under his bunk where crumpled tissues were thrown after he jerked off. Not one person during his twenty years in prison guessed that he would live with and love another man when finally released.

To Nick's relief, Padric McGarry was transferred into Cellblock 1-F, the homosexual area. 1-F was carefully guarded and segregated. At the intake, a captain who wore a girdle touched his arm.

You are better off with our own kind. Bend down. Spread your cheeks.

Sex in Dannemora: On the fly, in hallways, with the guy in the chapel, anyplace he could snatch three to five minutes.

He never had sex with all his clothes off. It was possible to have sex in the belfry. It was safe because it had a long, spiral stairway and even the lightest step on the stairway would ring because the steps were metal. Someone coming up the steps could be heard a mile away. The routine was to tell the guard that he was going up to sweep up the dead green flies, and to send 'Jerry' or another trick up with a mop. An all clear might mean five or ten minutes together.

He went to work in the prison tailor shop where he was taught to measure men by an old tailor, using a string he tied to his waist. As instructed, he measured around the neck and added one-half inch for wearing ease. He measured around the fullest part of the man's chest, used the string. To measure hips, he measured at the seat or the fullest part of the hip. He marked the tape position with pins on the undergarment and measured down from the waist using pins to establish a hipline. He noted the distance from waist to hip. Finally he measured the center back from the prominent neck bone to the waist string.

For sleeve length, he said, Bend your arm.

He measured across the man's shoulders from the base of the neck over elbow to wrist. For leg length, he measured from the waist down the outside of the leg to the knee and then to the floor or to the desired leg length. He notated both measurements, he was either getting a hard on by now or not. Then, the icing on the cake, to get crotch length, he sat on a hard, flat chair, measured from the side of the waist at the string to the chair seat. His busy, fussy fingers might stray.

After a while he was assigned to sew summer BVD's.

Wake up: Six a.m. Lights out: Nine p.m.

Affair: With Little Joey, doing fifty-to-life for murder. An icicle for a prick.

Marriage: To James Case Kelly, a "straight" man in another cellblock with fungus between his toes. Padric McGarry and James Case were "married" for more than a year. They never touched each other except on one occasion when they managed to brush knees.

Parole refused.

Red got discharged first.

Let's join forces, Pat.

I'll meet your train in New York when I get released.

He did the full five-year maximum sentence because all his job applications were rejected, and the parole board refused to accept the one or two that indicated lukewarm interest.

He was released on December 4, 1957. I'm an "old" man of thirty-two, was how he described himself.

He had a few drinks in Albany. Quickly drunk, he waited for the train to New York City, bought a flaming yellow silk scarf, tied it jauntily around his neck á la Amelia Earhart. On the train he divided people he saw into two groups – Mongrels or Pedigrees.

Through the train window, a blizzard was building. Often during the journey the flying snow obscured the scenery. He couldn't see Manhattan as the train approached, only fat snowflakes pasting across the glass.

When the train stopped at Grand Central Station, he got off, looked for Red but couldn't find him. He stood outside in the snow near the bronze statue of Commodore Cornelius Vanderbilt. The cold wasn't bad but it kept snowing. He waited for a few hours. He moved over to the Forty-Second Street entrance to the station below Mercury, Hercules and Minerva supporting the thirteen-foot clock until restlessness returned.

He retraced his steps and again waited inside Grand Central Station at the main concourse leaning against a great pier for a while longer. Above his head, he realized the vaulted ceiling was painted electric blue and illuminated with twinkling constellations of the far-away zodiac. Weak shafts of light stretched down from the seventy-five foot windows, almost like a picture postcard.

Red didn't show up. Outside Grand Central the steady but soft snow became a blizzard that dropped full-blown over the neighborhood, sending the snow upward, an icy wind raging.

At the first liquor store he bought a fifth of Old Crow.

He saw Beatniks in a bar on Sullivan Street.

He turned a trick at Sixth Avenue and Greenwich Avenue beside the Women's House of Detention. He heard a butch voice yelling up at the upper windows.

Sheila. Babe. No more pricks.

He met a whiskey salesman in a gay bar on Eighth Avenue. They found a hotel. Padric began to cough, kicked off his shoes. The whiskey salesman was a rock expert, showed him small samples of rocks, described the thin layers in shale, the coarse grain of sandstone, decomposed plant material in coal, and tiny, well-preserved and uncrushed fossils that he'd seen in fine-grained limestone. The salesman passed out. Padric robbed all his liquor samples but left his brown leather rock case on the radiator. He gave one of the whiskey samples (Boodles Gin) to a bum sitting on the stoop.

Who are you, brother? Robin Hood?

He encountered a sexual sadist.

He played the maracas in an after hours club.

He went down to the Bowery, had nothing to sell in the pawnshop, looked through the window into a barber school, walked past flophouses. He rented a room at The Sunshine Hotel and slept in an unventilated cubicle smaller than a prison cell. It had bedbugs in the mattress on which were rust stains. There was a locker in the cubicle and one light bulb hung from the ceiling covered with chicken-wire.

The second night he slept in a different flophouse. The guy at the desk handed him a small quantity of toilet paper when he paid for the room. The light in the room stayed on all through the night.

He told the desk clerk, I can't seem to make it on the outside.

He felt as if inevitably he'd be heading back to prison and the Bowery seemed like the most comfortable place to wait.

He went on the wagon, cleaned apartments to earn money. His hands got chafed from the cleaning fluid. He cleaned one near Columbus Circle next door to a shabby shop that was a treasure drove of second-hand junk, knickknacks, old clothes. The clothes were cheap, but he didn't buy any because he had nowhere to keep anything. He bought a pack of Kools from the United Cigar each afternoon when he finished work.

He found feathers in Central Park, he was sure they were from the swans. He loitered in the park.

He met Tracy Shore. He told Tracy about his life.

Stop drinking, Pat.

That's the least of my problems, Tracy.

He took odd jobs, was able to stay on the wagon. He didn't like to work, left every job as soon as he could.

On St. Patrick's Day he went to a bar. It was like a church. He looked at the shelf of bottles along the wall, the alter.

One drink.

Of?

Brandy.

He had an affair with Hal Benninghoven, an unemployed actor, some years younger than he was. Hal was diabetic, underweight, possessive, wrote poetry. Hal and he exchanged wedding rings.

He was hired by Mrs. Musgrove to look after her children. Hal came with him to North Carolina by train to meet his future boss in her summerhouse. The train went through the Great Smoky Mountains, though tunnels and high trestles, it wound through mountains. They groped each other when the train went into a tunnel and got pitch black. Hal showed him Blue Ridge Parkway, Grandfather Mountain.

It's six thousand feet.

Hal showed him Ashville, North Carolina, with the Vanderbilt's two hundred fifty-five room French Renaissance chateau, much too big to see everything. Padric couldn't find where the Musgove family lived, had lost the letter that had the address.

Hal sold his watch and they went to New Orleans by Greyhound. They couldn't afford a room at the Roosevelt Hotel but Hal could pay for a lunch of fried oysters on soft, doughy French bread although the peppers inside were so hot Padric spit his first bite back out.

We need to find a hotel.

Let's go to the French Quarter first, Hal, I want to see if anyone remembers me.

In this humidity?

It makes me sexy.

Let's leave New Orleans, Hal begged. You're drunk all the time and running around the Old Quarter.

Hal persuaded him to take a bus with him to Carlsbad, New Mexico.

In Carlsbad, New Mexico Hal took Padric to meet his mother who owned a motel. It was August 1958. They stayed in Carsbad for one month.

Padric robbed the mother's motel cash register. He snuck off to the bus station. No goodbyes.

He hocked his wedding ring and bought a bottle of sherry with the money.

Where are you from?

The Greyhound station.

No shit.

No, from Rikers Island actually.

His money was stolen from a cheap motel room. In a panic, he telephoned Hal.

Come.

Hal forged a withdrawal from his mother's bank account and got a bus.

Padric had stolen some sheer women's underwear, he'd plucked his eyebrows entirely out. After much to drink, Hal fell asleep. Padric picked Hal's pocket and got out of town. Alone.

At dawn he threw a brick through the glass door of a gas station. He wanted a Coke. He deposited a dime in the machine. The police apprehended him.

He served nine months in county jail.

Charge: Breaking and entering.

The only thing given him to read in county jail, old issues of *Gun & Ammo Magazine*. While inside he had a semi-mystical 'dream-vision' experience that he felt was connected with reincarnation.

He was released from prison. Hal was waiting for him. They took a bus to San Francisco, did menial jobs, all of which Padric hated.

Padric stole anything he could lay his hands on.

Hal tried to kill him.

Padric got a job in a department store but was caught stealing from the cash register.

You're fired.

Padric and Hal got back together.

Just before Christmas, they had a huge fight. Hal again tried to kill him.

January 1, 1960. He took a soggy, but moneyed John to a New Year's Eve party. Padric tried unsuccessfully to foist the John on a young queen.

You brought him you fuck him, Paddy.

He and the young queen, who had never seen one another before, stole a credit card from the drunken John. Padric charged liquor on it, forged the man's name, got rid of the young queen. He charged a shirt, forged the name. He made other charges on the card. All charges under $25. Total within a month: $800.

He picked up a sailor. The sailor took him home. After sex the sailor brewed up a pot of coffee. Padric made a smart crack and the sailor threw scalding coffee across his naked body. He fled, in agony.

Padric telephoned Tracy Shore.

I've stopped drinking.

Good.

Another arrest, county jail:

In jail, someone tipped him off that the police were after him for credit card forgeries.

Get far away as soon as you get out of here. If they catch you they'll throw away the key for all those forgeries.

When he was released he took a freight train from San Francisco to Seattle. Ugly red stubble was rough across his cheeks, a cloud of minute insects hid in his dirty hair. He looked up a buddy, Dan Boodey, stayed with Dan for a week, drank beer in the morning. When Dan went out to buy more beer, Padric left with all Dan's possessions.

He pawned what he'd stolen from Dan so he could drink in a Seattle gay bar, while looking for a John. He was arrested, was losing count of the number of arrests. Dan Boodey declined to press charges.

Charge: Soliciting for oral and anal sodomy.

Sentence: 180 days in Seattle County Jail

Seattle Country Jail. Padric was surrounded by AB'ers—Ayrian Brotherhood—with cloverleaf tattoos cut directly into the left sides of their chests with the numbers six six six inked over the cloverleaves.

White Box preached, Three sixes, the mark given by "the beast" son of Satan, the Antichrist, to the wicked. Book of Revelations, Chapter Thirteen, verses 16-18.

My ass.

White Box insisted, The Bible teaches white supremacy.

When he completed the Seattle sentence two officials took him to the San Francisco airport for extradition. Waiting for the plane, he was treated to lunch. He wolfed down his meal of meatloaf and mashed potatoes, and also the meal of one of the escorts, Swiss steak. It was his first plane ride.

Sentence: Seven-and-a-half to fourteen years. One year in psychiatric medical facility.

He was transferred to another California institution. He served one year—November 1960 – November 1961, at a psychiatric "medical" facility. He agreed to accept therapy. His job was to oversee a post-surgery recovery room in the prison hospital. He made friends with Miss Phoebe—Harold Feebleman—who was eighteen and worked in the ward among two hundred or more beds, many filled with men who had venereal diseases. Harold covered his long hair with a red cowboy bandana.

Feebleman? What a strange name. I read in the paper that men with odd names commit four times as many crimes as men with common names.

They do?

Yes.

My name has caused me embarrassment, I've been ridiculed.

See.

Yeah, but my name isn't that unusual.

He began to correspond with Tracy Shore. All his teeth were pulled and he was given an entire set of false teeth.

Late in 1961 he was transferred to another California institution where he had his own room and was called— for the first time in his entire life—Mr. McGarry.

Dear Tracy…
He began, but had nothing else to say that day.

Parole: October 1962.
He left the prison wearing a nylon, short-sleeve shirt

He took a freight train to El Paso, Texas.
A guy on the freight train with him got real close, a rotten stink came from his mouth.
Who is Lumumba?
I have no idea. A dance?

He stood at Santa Fe Port of Entry into Ciudad Juarez, Mexico, but did not know what to do to cross over into Mexico. He walked back downtown.
A soldier told him, If you want to go to Mexico, catch the bus at the corner of Paisano and Stanton. It says, PTE LIBRE.
Padric asked, Wanna go?
I got to be back at Fort Bliss at four.

Who's to fight down there? Geronimo, Pancho Villa. Do you like beer?

It's just I'm broke.

Is there any Bliss at Fort Bliss?

The soldier didn't get the joke.

He hopped a freight to Los Angeles.

He turned a trick with an old John.

I'll take you to the Grauman's Chinese Egyptian Theater.

The taxi dropped them at the sidewalk at gray terrazzo circles embedded by pink stars, at Burt Lancaster's star. The John went to search for Marilyn Monroe's star and Padric went off to find Marlon Brando. The John sprung for highballs at the Biltmore.

Come on to Frederick's of Hollywood, just up the street. I'll buy you underwear and things.

Padric said, No.

He got a job as desk clerk in a hotel run by the Salvation Army, in Santa Ana, California. Miss Phoebe visited him at the hotel. They drank together.

Drive back to New York with me, oh please.

In what?

I'll steal us a great car.

Padric remembered a car he'd seen with a medallion of a bird that hurled bolts of lightning with its talons. He described it to Miss Phoebe.

Padric stole a bundle of clothes from the Salvation Army warehouse. Among them a green and orange striped dress. Miss Phoebe picked him up in the stolen car.

It has front wheel drive, Miss Phoebe bragged.

What is it?

An almost new 1962 Thunderbird.

Padric looked for the porthole windows, the external spare tire, the lightning bolts from the birds talons.

Phoebe saw his disappointment.

It's not a two-seat *boulevardier*. Ours has textured grill instead "dual pod." I like less flash, I like chrome ornamentation. Zero to sixty in 10.4. I'm not garish at all.

And I am … from Bronx, New York?

They filled the trunk with the stolen clothes.

They stopped for gas in Phoenix and got into a fight with a gas station attendant.

They abandoned the car with all the clothes in the trunk.

They hopped a freight train outside of Phoenix going east.

In El Paso, Texas, two bulls boarded the freight train and gathered all the riders. Padric was arrested. The cop bragged about El Paso as they waited for the paddy wagon, John Wesley Hardin, buried in Concordia Cemetery, El Paso, near Boot Hill, killed forty people with a six shooter.

Crime: Transporting a stolen vehicle across state lines.

Sentence: Under Dyer Act, three years in the Federal Penitentiary. Miss Phoebe was a minor, got taken to another institution for sentencing.

He arrived at Leavenworth in November 1962. Leavenworth had a sentry box with mounted machine guns. Leavenworth, U.S. Penitentiary, in Leavenworth, Kansas, close to the Missouri River made of concrete and steel, with a dome. He was fingerprinted and photographed, was left in a waiting room that had old spittoons and oak desks. He was not segregated from the heterosexual prisoners.

There were five inmate counts a day: At ten p.m. when the inmates were locked in for the night, at midnight, at three a.m., at five thirty a.m. and every day at four p.m. when the prisoners returned to their cells from work for the fifth count of the day. His cell was five and a half by nine.

He got a job in the prison's clothing factory where he was assigned an industrial sewing machine in the center of a long row of sewing machines. He got serious about perfecting his sewing skill: He mastered the straight stitch, zigzag stitch, chain or decorative stitch. He never let his bobbin get empty, and never wound new thread on a partially filled bobbin. He became famous as a hotshot with the zipper foot for zipper insertions, corded seams. He requisitioned for some optional attachments. He asked for a buttonholer, a ruffler, and a tucker but none arrived due to budget cuts.

He interfered in an argument between two inmates and was stabbed in an ensuing brawl.

He earned two hundred dollars in government bonds working at the clothing factory. On sunny afternoons, the sun bled through the cathedral-sized windows in the cellhouse. A gray shadow in the shape of a grid crisscrossed the tile floor.

He was paroled in May 1965 after serving two and a half years, walked out through the electronic gate.

He got on a bus, went cross country to New York on Mother's Day, 1965.

His legs hurt after three days of sitting when he got off the bus in New York at the Greyhound Station.

He sat on a red plastic barstool at the Terminal Bar on Eighth Avenue.

A double bull and ball.

He sank the shot glass into the beer, felt butch.

He walked over to visit Tracy Shore's apartment stinking of whiskey, looked up at Tracy's window. The window was dark, the front door of the building had frosted glass panels that he couldn't see into.

He took the subway down to the Bowery, wandered past a row of restaurant supply shops, also a mission. He sat on a loading platform to think but a Chinese bum began to speak to him in Chinese. He walked until the Manhattan Bridge rose up in a triumphal arch, curved colonnade, a gateway to the end of the world.

He walked north, found himself on Clinton Street. It soon turned into Avenue B. He took the red and yellow Avenue B bus that crossed Fourteenth Street but it terminated at Klein's Department Store. He got off and walked south down Fourth Avenue.

He walked back past jewelry shops selling only diamonds, past the Salvation Army Hotel at 225. He drank up the last of his two hundred dollars.

He woke up in a flophouse on the Bowery, flooded with gusts of anxiety, quickly counted his remaining money. Only small change was left. He had red bristles on his cheeks that were raw from a two dollar blow job. He went to the Bowery Bar and ordered a drink with the remaining coins.

When he was totally broke, he traded his teeth with another bum for a bottle of "dago red" muscatel.

Toothless, he hitched to upstate New York where he got a job washing dishes in a restaurant. Within a week he was accused of stealing from the register and from the tip cup, was fired and paid off.

Padric spent the night in the bushes. He was drunk. He shoplifted beer and a carton of Kool from a small market.

Arrest: Sixty days, felony tank, city jail, upstate New York. The crime: Shoplifting.

In the felony tank of the county jail in upstate New York, June 1965, he wrote with turquoise ink to Tracy Shore:

I was sitting in my cell, it was the same old kind of cell, it was sunny that day and I could hear children's voices from a park outside. And I was annoyed by the slap-bang of dominoes in a game two of the guards were playing out in the corridor. I was just sitting there, staring at the gray wall, when I fell down suddenly into the worst feeling I've ever had. It was like I could see, for the first time ever, a terrible, dreary pattern in my whole life. I was so tired of cells. Way down in my belly I began to scream. It got very quiet, I don't think I could hear the children or the dominoes anymore. Then everything in the cell got bright. I left my body and walked to the back of the cell and looked at myself. I could see me sitting there on the bed but then it turned into this big sieve all covered with filth and grease and dirt until the sieve began to slowly get clean and bright and transformed itself back into my body. I re-entered it. I felt light. I felt clean. I banged on the bar with my cup for the hack. I got paper and pencil and started writing to you.

Tracy wrote back,

Glad to hear from you again. It does indeed sound like something good and new has come into your life. I'll be glad to see you if and when you come to New York.

Tracy

He was transferred to Lewisburg Federal Penitentiary in July via New York. En route he was placed in the Federal House of Detention in the West Village. They gave him a haircut that looked like a lawnmower had been pushed across his scalp. Sharing his cell, an old queen, La La Ken, with a tattoo of Mickey Mouse drooping across his sagging chest. La La never let go of his prick, touched and checked that it was still there night and day.

Tracy visited. They had met face-to-face seven years before but Padric hadn't remembered that he had such a lean and earnest face, eyes like ripe blackberries. Tracy gave him ten dollars.

I owe six months on my federal sentence.

Why?

I violated my parole.

The transfer to Lewisburg was completed.

In Lewisburg, Padric received a letter from Tracy:

I'll support you for two weeks after your release if you promise to do nothing but go to AA meetings around the clock during the first week, and will begin to look for a job and make plans during the second week. I'm making this offer for my own sake. Not yours.

Padric set up an appointment with the dentist to be fitted for new false teeth—upper and lower plates—hoping it could be done before he was released. It was done along with the removal of a nerve that wriggled and twitched between the bloody prongs of the dentist's tweezers.

He attended fifty-six AA meetings during thirty days. Tracy arranged for an AA guy to get him a dirt cheap apartment on Seventeenth Street at Ninth Avenue, a small single on an inside courtyard with no window onto the street, just a window into the courtyard and a big bathtub that stood on bent legs with clawed feet in the livingroom. The apartment had once belonged to the super and had access to the basement of the building. The guy gave him the key to the door.

Don't lose it, it's the only one.

Padric made a fist over the key.

I'm a remarkable person, he told the guy, I never lost a key in my life.

He didn't mention that he'd never possessed one either.

He fell in the snow on Eighth Avenue spraining his ankle so he stayed off his feet.

He caught cold. Stayed in bed all day.

He manicured his finger and toenails with tools in a kit—pushed the cuticles with the little stick, applied clear polish. He needed a haircut but didn't get one, just let his hair grow and grow.

AA people gave him pots and pans, utensils, two drinking glasses, mustard, velvet drapes.

He invited Tracy by for lunch and made deviled eggs and served canned pears.

He stole a Clairol kit from Woolworth's and dyed his hair flaming red.

Mind you, he told the AA home group the first time he spoke at a meeting, I haven't stopped stealing but I'm more careful about it.

He found an occasional paying John, had frequent sexual encounters in his neighborhood. He performed by rote. Sex was flat. He couldn't always keep his mind on what he was doing, his thoughts often drifted. He turned some tricks with older men in AA.

He came down with chicken pox, was told, It'll make you sterile.

First job: He delivered lunches for a seafood restaurant. He delivered fried clams to a lady wearing a housedress who asked him to run down and buy her a bottle of A-1 Sauce. At the end of the day he could still smell seafood on his clothes. He hated it.

Second job: In a small accessory boutique, he washed the floor with cleaning fluid. At the end of the day his clothes and hair stank of cleaning fluid. He hated it.

Third job: As an apprentice in a tailor shop. The tailor drank milk all day and smelled like sour milk. Padric mastered the art of making patches. He already knew how to hem, and could do just about anything else with a needle and thread. He hated working at a job.

He went to a Turkish bath. He met Michael Morris and they began an affair. Michael gave him a gold locket and a twenty dollar bill. Padric bought a camel's-hair coat at a thrift shop for fifteen dollars. He looked like a millionaire from the neck down when he saw himself passing a reflecting shop window, he imagined he looked like Veronica Lake from the neck up—the hair, the way he could fling it around. He had a feeling, not that he'd go back to drinking, but that something he couldn't name was going to happen—like a tooth ache that doesn't really hurt a lot but is always there.

Michael wanted to get him out of the neighborhood, wanted to better him. He took him uptown on Friday night to Second Avenue and Seventy-Fourth Street to a bar called Dr. Generosity's that gave away free penny candy. Padric drank straight tonic with a squeeze of lime, Michael slowly sipped a wine spritzer. They walked into another bar, called Maxwell's Plum filled with people who looked like they worked in offices. Michael ordered another wine spritzer. Padric didn't know what to order, it seemed stupid to pay for a soft drink. He refused.

He heard the bartender say, Get *her*!

Michael lowered the TV, opened the curtains. Padric lit another cigarette, broke open a box of Uneeda Biscuits.

Why do I always have to initiate lovemaking? Michael asked.

Padric put a pillow under Michael's ass.

What are you watching, Michael?

The Orange Bowl.

Padric seasoned chicken wings with lots of salt and pepper and paprika. He broiled the wings in silver foil and set them in a bowl on the coffee table.

He got involved with the Dismas Association and appeared on a TV show in the summer of 1967, had refused to cut his hair before the show.

Why should I? My hair is thick and Irish, it has lots of body. My last crowning glory.

He wore a red and white polo shirt, green shorts, and got a tiny gold ring inserted into his right ear a few days before the show.

From *The New York Times*, July 13, 1967—*2 Ex-Convicts, Onstage, Tell of "Living Hell". Former Junkie and Burglar on Actors Playhouse Panel... What an unreal world, Piri Thomas moaned at the silent faces staring up at him from the audience, Man, what an unreal world." Piri Thomas, the author of* Down These Mean Streets, *a critically praised autobiographical book, was talking about prison and the six years he spent in one. Seated next to him on the stage of the tiny Actors Playhouse in Sheridan Square, Pat McGarry, who has spent 25 of his 42 years in various prisons, nodded gently as Mr. Thomas—snapping his fingers for emphasis and breaking into his own thoughts to ask, Am I telling it right, my man?—bellowed and wailed at the "living hell" called prison. Mr. Thomas put it simply and directly: The homosexual in prison does the worst time of all, he said, I've seen them beaten, slashed, kicked—the whole bit. Mr. McGarry, a tall, thin, self-described homosexual and ex-burglar had high praise for the California prison system, where he said prisoners were fed decently, called "mister" by guards. Mr. Thomas said, A convict is the next best thing to a dead man. Mr. McGarry was not so sure. He recalled that when he came up for parole when in Clinton Prison at Dannemora, N.Y., on a 2 1/2-to-6 year sentence for burglary, the first thing the parole board asked him was whether he was a homosexual. I said yes, and they said we'll see you next time. I did every day of those five years.*

He got a job as a general apprentice to a theatrical costume house. He was happy. He loved this job, and excelled. Everyone loved him, he made people laugh. He was funny, camped at everything.

He didn't have one drink in nine years. He got a green parakeet. He named her Miss Scarlet and spent every extra penny he got his hands on at thrift shops on Ninth Avenue.

Framed on his kitchenette wall:

HOMO NEST RAIDED,

QUEEN BEES ARE STINGING MAD.

Miss Scarlet flew out the door as Padric cleaned his cage. When he ran into the street the trees were drooping from so much rain but the bird was gone. Miss Scarlet was never seen again.

He went to an AA meeting in the big church at Houston and Sullivan. He opened the wrong door, climbed up some steps, and found himself above an alter near to which an organ was being played by a woman. Below him was a girl about nineteen tossing her hair with coquetry, walking solemnly toward the alter holding the arm of a mustached man wearing a white flower on his lapel. At the altar, the priest's back was turned, the organ played "Here Comes The Bride." Seven or eight people seated in the front two pews were twisting their heads around to watch the procession. Looking down at the wedding he felt indifference toward the couple but an attraction for the priest.

He was very hungry, skipped the AA meeting and found a booth at the Greek coffee shop off Sheridan Square. He counted the money in his little squeegee purse. He didn't have enough for the corned beef and cabbage special but had enough for French toast and gave his order.

Extra butter and extra syrup, thanks Hon.

The waiter knew him. Kidded him, called him "Aunt Mary."

He slathered syrup and whipped butter onto all four slices of battered bread and let them melt together. He didn't have enough money left for hair color, his next paycheck wouldn't come until Friday, so he smartly shoplifted "Fire Engine Red" hair dye along with a Mars Bar and white thread from Rexall Drugs.

He took a costume or two home from the costume house, rationalizing that he was just 'borrowing' them temporarily. He took others, had become a compulsive thief.

He was caught stealing. Nothing was said. A week later he was fired. He wasn't prosecuted.

He took a job as a porter at a Broadway theater. Every day—thick red mane boastfully flying, cashmere coat buttoned—he floated up Eighth Avenue with noiseless footsteps, past Forty-Second and Eighth, past young, lanky hustlers.

He threw little comments their way: Mornin' girls. How's tricks? Nice buns ya' got. If you kiss my elbow, you'll turn into a member of the opposite sex, haha.

When he got to the theater he changed out of his good shoes into sneakers, relieving his chronic heel pain.

In 1969 he received an offer made by a friend he'd met in the Dismas Association. Hank wanted to set him up in a boutique.

I'll supply the capital and you'll supply the taste, talent, and manage it.

It was a dream come true. He worked hard setting up the shop and didn't touch a dime of Hank's money.

The morning after the Grand Opening, Hank telephoned.

I won't need you after all. I need more capital so I've brought in someone else who has cash.

To Padric's surprise he took the blow in stride. He bought himself a second-hand watch fob at a thrift shop. Outside the shop, wearing brown overalls, good looking, beefy men lifted heavy furniture wrapped in green protective moving blankets. He pocketed the watchless fob.

A silky, white cat with elegant paws ran from the basement up into his apartment, jumped onto the kitchen counter and howled for food.

Padric shared his cache of raw chopped meat with the cat.

The cat grew very fat. His white fur got dingy gray where it brushed against the cellar stairs. He was named Serenity.

Someone in AA gave Padric a little potted cactus plant.

He tasted figs.

He tasted curry.

He ate in a Japanese restaurant.

He had a boyfriend who owned a 1969 Cougar Mercury, wore Aqua Velva After Shave, and took him for a drive to the Jersey Shore.

They watched Pope Paul VI on TV as his helicopter whirled up from a stadium somewhere in Africa. The helicopter seat on which the Pope sat was like a throne.

The ceramic ashtray he'd lifted from Schrafft's stank of nicotine.

He bought a pink and turquoise kimono from Chinatown. It was new, not second-hand.

His favorite snack:

He would line up Jacob's Cream Crackers on a baking tray and put a marshmallow on top of each one. Then, a small pat of butter onto the marshmallow. Finally, a blanched almond into the butter. He put the baking tray into the stove until the marshmallow had melted all over the biscuits.

His favorite light supper:

He peeled two large onions and put them in his baking tin. He added about an inch of water and let them bake for about an hour, sometimes two. Periodically he'd open the oven, squeeze the onions. When they were soft he'd take them out, pull back the brown skin and cut off the root. He added a pat of butter, salt and pepper.

His favorite midnight snack:

He'd combine warm mashed potatoes and oatmeal into soft dough. He'd add salt and melted butter or bacon drippings (which he rarely had, bacon being so expensive). He rolled the mix out like dough and cut it into rounds or triangles, then fried them on both sides with more butter.

Full of fat, jumping, summer fleas, he gathered ingredients together to rid Serenity of the pests:

1 cup rice baby cereal which he pre-mixed with water

1 cup strained turkey baby food

1/2 cup low-fat cottage cheese

1/4 clove fresh-roasted garlic.

He divided the glop into four meals, wrapped them separately in Saran. He had a hard time coaxing Serenity to even eat because she was scratching so much.

First heart attack: 1972

On the day of his release from the cardiac unit at Bellevue, the doctor drew with a Papermate on his prescription pad. He sketched a heart, valves, and veins, arteries, explained:

The left ventricle of the heart pumps blood into the aorta, a very large artery. The healthy aorta is about one inch in diameter. It curves up, arching, then runs down the back of your chest and abdominal cavity. It divides in two. Two arteries. One supplies your legs, one supplies your pelvic region, and organs with the blood they need.

The doctor drew another diagram, added arrows. Padric listened.

And my groin?

He qualified for SSI.

Good. I'll never have to work another day in my life!

He likened himself to a bear with a big silver fish in his mouth.

He telephoned Michael.

Guess what? John Mitchell walked out on Martha. She set fire to his war medals and hockey mementoes.

No shit, Sherlock.

Michael slammed down the telephone.

Sick cow.

All dressed up. Nowhere to go.

Cloudless sky.

Great thirst:

Glass of cold water.

Glass of Pepsi.

Glass of V-8.

Glass of ice tea.

Glass of lime-ade.

Cup of hot white tea in the afternoon.

Cup of Postum at night.

A small glass of prune juice on waking.

Second heart attack:

Early in the week Tom B. from AA called to know if he had a costume he could borrow to wear to a drag ball on Fire Island.

Tom told him, I've never done drag before.

Tom was a big, truck-driver-shaped man, very pleasant, had phoned because Padric was tall as he was, over six feet.

Tom arrived at seven o'clock. Padric had been down in the basement looking through the boxes of stolen costumes and clothes. He found a few things and brought them upstairs. Tom wanted to dress as an elderly, respectable Irish lady. They were in the process of going through the things he'd brought up when Padric remembered something else, a lovely Jurex black and silver caftan-type dress that covered a multitude of sins. He also recalled a wig, a beautiful red wig, he thought would flatter Tom. Also gloves, jewelry, a magnificent cape done in sequins and black fox collar and velvet. All fit Tom perfectly except he couldn't find shoes since Tom wore size thirteen. So, again and again, Padric ran down the basement stairway, and up again.

Tom left about eight-thirty, left Padric sitting on the bed. Quite soon he began to feel pain, first he felt it in his chest, then it went into his arm that was, he consciously thought, a sign that another heart attack was coming. Could it be? It was sharp, like a knife in the bone, a wound that began to crawl up and across his chest from his arm toward the base of his neck. He began to choke.

The pain went up the neck to the jaw and his skull bones felt as though they were being crushed.

He just sat. He considered calling the hospital or 911 and thought, No, if I'm going to die, please let me die. Then he remembered some phenobarbitol from his 1972 heart attack. He forced himself off the bed and into the bathroom, got the pheno pills, took two, and went and sat down.

He said to his cat, Alright Serenity, it doesn't matter. It doesn't matter. Either I'll die or I'll get better.

Then he stretched out while Serenity watched and listened, sat beside him. As Padric felt worse and worse, Serenity purred deeply.

The cat rubbed up against his shoulder and was looking at him, purring silkily.

Padric began to go. He was ready.

I've had enough.

He got drowsy, fell sleep, the tip of his fingers touching Serenity's fur.

While Padric convalesced, an AA friend brought him books by Jane Roberts, an American woman who'd contacted entities through using the Ouija board. He flipped. Jane's teacher called himself "Seth" and he read everything he could find about or by her.

After reading these books he told Serenity, I am God individualized. I am God experiencing itself. I am eternal. I chose my own parent—with their consent—as an entree to the earth plane...

Serenity turned away, strolled into the bathroom and scratched in the magenta plastic kitty litter box.

Morning:
He soaked six dates in a Tupperware bowl filled with warm water. He chewed each one well, sipped the water.

Before bed:
He took two teaspoons of apple cider vinegar in a glass of warm water.

He was dressed to fly in an airplane, the second flight of his life, a true miracle. He had a pristine passport that had taken months to get because of his record. The ticket, a gift from eleven AA friends. Elated, he talked nonstop to the Catholic nun next to him for seven hours while crossing the North Atlantic.

Dawn came quickly, the night collapsed down. In London he changed planes. From the air, he saw land, then hills, water, slopes, pinnacles, towers, spires, a spangled green river mouth, earth coming toward him. He used mouthwash and gargled, plumped his long, red hair.

He experienced gross confusion at the airport.

How do I get into Glasgow, Sir? How do I find the bus station, Madam?

He couldn't understand one word spoken to him in reply. One gent took him by the arm, walked him to a bus, gave him a little push aboard.

The bus went alongside the M8 motorway and dropped him at Buchanan Bus Station. Paul was waiting to take him to Dalmeny Guest House on St. Andrews Drive three miles away. Paul had a florid face, a full, black beard like Paul Bunyon. Padric wanted to squeeze him, but didn't dare touch except for reciprocating the bear hugs that Paul initiated.

Paul kept grinning as Padric ate. And ate. He ate every last tasty scrap.

Paul informed him, with glee, It's sheep's stomach stuffed with minced heart, liver and lungs, along with suet, onions and oatmeal. It's called haggis. Was it piping hot enough?

In the morning, under a leaden sky, they left for Findhorn.

Dear Benefactors,

I didn't say anything about my identity to the group on this first day and no one asked. Rain.

Dear Benefactors,

Rain.

Dear Benefactors,

The gardens are planted on sand. I realized that I was born into the wrong time and wrong place. Although nothing but hardy Scottish bushes and grasses usually grow here, as a result of members telepathic communication with Angelic Beings and instructions communicated by Angelic Beings back, tropical plants unheard of in Scotland, unheard of in winter anywhere, grow. 40 pound cabbages. People explained that all life is an outpost or point of entry through which great intelligence can externalize itself. "Shining ones" or "devics" or "devas" are the transmitters. But, swallow this, we are children of the vast reaches of space. Never underestimate what we are. Tap your "devic" essences.

More rain. Oh, and they don't kill maggots on the cabbages, or shoo rabbits or moles or birds away. All are welcome and the vegetables are huge and eatable too.

Dear Benefactors,

I am where God means me to be. I AM power. I work every day in the garden, laying manure down. I can still carry large bags on my back and weld a heavy shovel but not all day like I once did or twirl it like a baton. Still no letters from any of you benefactors, no rain for 3 days, but always threatening.

Sex no longer rules me. The Atomic Bomb is nothing compared to the power of my own dreams. But, how can I handle Godliness, if I cannot handle my own personality? My own sex drive? I've come to understand that my personality is consciousness bound and determined by form, my Godliness is consciousness—boundless and self-determining—through my link to all nature and even the stars in the heavens. What a mouthful!

It will be terrible to leave here because I'm thriving. Except for a few "personalities" I have no problems with anyone though I haven't discussed being gay. I can't imagine they don't know. The subject just hasn't come up. No one has commented on my hair. For or against.

The only way I'll be able to get myself to pack and say goodbye on Monday will be knowing that I will return. Somehow. With God as my witness (picture Scarlet O'Hara, a handful of carrots in her hand shaking her fist at the world), I'll return and live here. I'm home.

He began to knit an afghan bedspread. His choice of yarn—pink, turquoise and white. He could make a large can of Chef Boy-ar-dee Ravioli (twenty-six ounces) last for five meals.

He bought a little bouquet of grayish, greenish pearled mistletoe and hung it over his doorway before Christmas. He left it there after Christmas, let it turn golden, because it could stimulate fertility and might avert ulcers.

He learned to make risotto.

Travel books borrowed from the library:
On Tierra Del Fuego
On Timbuktu
On Christmas Island
On Greenland
On Andorra
On the Faroe Islands
On Khabarovsk.

Straining to see, farsighted recently, he held the gay rural magazine at arms length in order to read the Love-lorn Column.

MAIL ORDER BRIDE WANTED BY BUTCH WM IN OZARKS.

Will pay expenses. Object – Matrimony. Send photo and intention.

Padric went to a second-hand bookshop on Waverly Place and bought both volumes of *The Columbia Viking Desk Encyclopedia*. Second edition, revised and enlarged, 1960, for one dollar.

Ozark Mountains dissected plateau c. 50,000 sq. mi., chiefly in Mo. but partly in Ark., Okla. and Kansas lying between Arkansas and Missouri Rivers. Average 2,000 ft. in altitude, plateau slopes gently into the plains. Boston Mountains are highest, most rugged sector. Minerals (lead, zinc) are present. There is some fruit growing. Scenery, forests and mineral springs make region a resort. Ozark Lake. Central Mo. Created by Bagnell Dam in Osage R., it is c.130 m. long and of irregular shape. The lake offers numerous recreation facilities.

Arkansas, state, 52,725 sq. mi., Pop. 1,909,511, S. central U.S., admitted 1836 as 25th state, slaveholding; cap. Little Rock. Other major cities are Fort Smith, Pine Bluff, Hot Springs, Texarkana. Bounded on E. by Mississippi R., Mississippi alluvial plains S. and E; Ozark Mountains in NW. Has Arkansas R., St. Francis R., White River, Quachita R., Red River. Produces cotton, corn, rice, grains, truck, livestock, timber, petroleum, bauxite, coal. Industries based on processing of raw materials. Quapaw Indians lived here. Hernando De Soto led first white men into region in 1541-42. Trading center at Arkansas Post estab. by French 1686. Part of French territory, region was ceded to Spain (1762) and back to France before going to U.S. in Louisiana Purchase. 1818 cotton boom brought many settlers. Became territory 1819. Joined Confederacy 1861. State not readmitted to Union until 1868. Reconstruction turbulent. Depression of 1930s hit cotton economy hard, causing much migration (esp. to Calif.). World War II caused further population loss, also boomed new industries (esp. aluminum). Desegregation issue loomed large in 1954. Conflict between Federal and state authorities was especially tense in 1957-8 after Pres. Eisenhower sent Federal troops to Little Rock.

Bridal wreath: see Spiraea.

Bride, Saint: See Bridget, Saint.

Mail: See Postal Service.

Postal service, arrangement for delivering letters, packages, and periodicals. Courier systems for government use existed under the Persian Empire. Britain's postal service, an outgrowth of royal courier routes, was estab. finally in 1657 and penny postage (see Postage stamp) was begun in 1839. The U.S. system was derived from the colonial service established by England. In the U.S. postage stamps were first used 1847, registered mail 1855, city delivery 1863, money orders 1864, penny post cards 1873, special delivery 1885, rural delivery 1896, postal savings 1911, parcel post 1913. The pony express operated across the continent, 1960-61, rail service was instituted in 1862, air mail in 1918. The Universal Postal Union was established after the International Postal Convention of 1874.

Butch: no listing.

Expenses: no listing.

He went back to the bookshop and bought *Webster's College Dictionary* for nine dollars.

Butch: adj. 1. Slang. a. (of a woman) having traits of behavior, dress, etc. usu. associated with males. b. (of a male) exaggeratedly masculine in appearance or manner. 2. of or designating a haircut in which the hair is closely cropped. n. 3. Slang. a butch person (1940-1945; appar. from the proper name). Butcher. Butcherbird. Butcherblock. Butcherlinen. Butcherly. Butchersbroom. Butchery.

Bride: n. a newly married woman or a woman about to be married. Brideless. Bridelike. Bridal. Bridal wreath. Bridegroom. Brideprice. Bridesmaid. Bridewell.

He found a photo that Miss Phoebe had taken of him in Santa Ana. His face in profile against iron-gray cinderblocks of the Salvation Army building. He hoped that he looked like Bette Davis in *Dark Victory*.

He answered the ad, sent that photo and other information requested to the RR in Arkansas.

A one-way Greyhound bus ticket to the Ozarks slipped from the manila envelope, also hand-written instructions on how to go the forty-seven miles from the Greyhound bus station to the RR address.

He sold everything he'd acquired.

Friends warned: Don't give up your apartment whatever you do!

His reply: I can't live there another minute anyhow. No window. No air. No space. No light. I need a separate bedroom. A real kitchen.

More warnings: You'll never get anything at such a price.

He gave up the apartment.

He dropped the work he was doing on his biography with the green young girl from the East Side. He went to the SSI office, submitted a change of address so that his check for two hundred twenty-eight dollars per month would be forwarded.

He picked a new color for his hair. Less henna, more peachy.

Tracy took Serenity.

You must understand, Serenity. I must get out of this city. It's killing me. I must have a home, a husband, a normal life. I'll send for you...

A ball of gas swelled inside his stomach.

Serenity walked away, bared his claws and began to sharpen them on the maple leg of Tracy's sofa.

He left the stripped apartment at Seventeenth Street by taxi for the Port Authority Bus Station. The taxi went up Eighth Avenue past the belly dancing joints and dropped him on the corner of Fortieth. He gave the driver a two dollar tip.

The bus curled down the ramp, bypassed Forty-Second Street, was in the Lincoln Tunnel before he had even covered his legs with the turquoise, pink and white afghan throw he'd worked on for so long.

The bus rolled past low, sloping mountains, tall tulip poplars and white oaks, hickories, hard maples, cedars, pines, hemlocks and chestnuts. Also sycamores, lazy streams.

He fell asleep and when he woke a woman and a boy and many bundles were squeezed into the seat across the aisle.

The boy recited the same thing over and over:

Bob-o-link! Bob-o-link!

Spink! Spank! Spink!

The sloping road darkened with shadow, and it got very dark.

Padric thought, Oh please.

Near to the Greyhound Depot was a huge telescope into which anyone could study the planets and heavens. Padric consulted the instructions he'd been given: *Go to filling station on Route 1. On Tuesday and Thursday our mailman Ek Bater delivers mail in the green mail van to our neck of the woods. Be there by 8 and he'll take you the whole way. He knows us.*

Us?

It was Monday, three in the afternoon so he took a room at the William Finley Motel for sixteen dollars. He ate chicken fried steak with a double order of fries at the café. The meal tasted delicious, gooey, greasy, salty, peppery, starchy, everything he had been ordered by his cardiologist not to eat. He craved these foods, heart disease or no heart disease.

Where you going? the counterman who had a birthmark across his right cheek asked.

Home to Tara. Home to Mammy and Tara.

The counterman asked, When?

Tomorrow.

That's some fiery hair ya got.

That's some delicious looking apple pie ya got, can you heat it up and put a scoop of vanilla ice cream on the top?

Sure.

And maybe turn up that radio y'all got thar.

He took off his jacket.

Sure. Ya'll like country music?

Sure do darlin'. How far is the filling station from heah?

It's yonder, not five minutes past the barber shop on 1.

And two last questions. Could you keep my trunk heah foh me and I'll come an fetch it or send someone for it in a couple of days?

I don't know why not. It won't hurt nuthin'. What's the other question?

Can I buy the whole pie from hew? Hew got a box for me to carry it yonder?

Ah sure do. What are those scars up and down the inside of your arms mistah?

Mosquito bites. My mother told me not to scratch them but I did.

At dawn he dragged his suitcase down the black tar road, the cosmetic bag, the piece of hand luggage, the pie box, the afghan throw. Mist was thick and he couldn't see what was ahead. The filling station had one pump. He stopped and rested on his suitcase. His chest hurt. He counted his money again, hoping that the foggy dew wouldn't make his hair lank. He needed to shit but that could wait since there didn't seem to be a toilet in back of the filling station. He saw stands of frail, six inch irises some weighted down by pink slugs, realized he was across from a cemetery with markers made of field stones.

Ek wore a mesh fishing vest with zippers, a cloche hat. He carried mail and packages, also his fishing rod.

Ek dropped Padric at a mailbox on the road. He followed the dirt road that led up a rocky hill to the trailer Ek had pointed to, actually two trailers standing side by side.

Padric left everything but the pie box at the mailbox, and knocked on the door of the larger trailer, the one on cement blocks. The door opened. Padric pushed the boxed apple pie inside.

That ain't your real color hair, ain't it fake?

The voice didn't sound pleased to see him. Dickey was small, five fourish, pointed ears like a fawn, had cold, gray, mountain-man eyes.

My red badge of courage, Padric joked.

He bent his head, came inside, sank onto a sagging brown armchair, making a mental note to cover the ugly chair with the afghan. He put the pie box on top of the TV.

It ain't your real color? So what's the real color?

He remembered Scarlet talking to the tiresome Tarleton brothers.

If you say "real color" once more I'll scream. Why two trailers? His and his? Haha.

No. Mine and Ma's. Ma lives in the small one. She can't stand Italians, Irish, Jews, Niggers, Foreigners, Red Indians, Yankees, Queers or Catholics.

Padric's eyes scanned the trailer. His head scraped its ceiling when he stood straight. He kneeled in front of Dickey.

Aren't you happy? I am, darling. Your mail order bride has come heah to wed you.

He buried his face in Dickey's stiff corduroy lap. His heart was thumping very hard. He had to shit even worse. There didn't seem to be a bathroom in this miniature house. From nowhere, a big dog leapt onto his back. The old fear of dogs made him jump.

Dickey got stiff as a rod and didn't say anything else until after he got a blow job.

Non-stop constipation. The trailer smelled like a wet dog. The water was pumped outside. All morning long mist rose around the trailer and the clumps of trees and raspberry bushes.

A man came to fix the roof. He talked non-stop about Jesus Christ and Russian Devils.

The wedding was in Memphis, in a gay bar that had country and western dancing on Monday and Tuesday nights between eight and nine. Dickey brought his dog as best "friend." Padric had his hair refashioned. Ma was home in bed with arthritis. Padric's dream of kneeling side-by-side in front of an alter didn't materialize.

Dickey leaned against the screen door as Padric dropped a ham hock into the soup pot that was too big for the hot plate. He poured in water. He removed the soup pot, put it on top of the TV set, wiped out bits of fried egg from the skillet. He sang Ethel Merman doing "Some People" from *Gypsy* in falsetto as the bacon browned.

Dickey swatted flies.

Ma parcooked collards next door, the smell mingled with the smell of dog.

Padric poured bacon fat into an empty green pea can.

Don't drain the fat. Don't sing like that, Ma can hear through the wall.

Padric let the fat jump. He added chopped onions. He went out and smoked an L&M, then walked back in. He returned the soup pot to the burner, and threw in the mess from the frying pan. He added a chicken bouillon cube, a handful of sugar, black pepper, handfuls of their own collard greens and covered the pot.

Did you wash your hands before sticking them into the sugar bowl?

He slammed the screen door. His chest felt like it was encased in a strong rubber band. Since the second heart attack, he got a lump in his throat so easily, like a fool. Just wait till Dickey tasted his ham. He lit three forbidden cigarettes in a row.

Ma wasn't old at all. Hardly more than forty but was crooked with arthritis. Her pocketbook hung from the crook of her arm. She smelled like tobacco, also brought a sweet smell, like powder, with her, into Dickey's windowless cellish trailer.

Trash and leaves need dumping.

She thrust a recipe at Dickey.

Sunday. Church.

She let the screen door snap shut.

Dickey handed the recipe to Padric:

Bible cake: Answer the following questions and you will have the proper amounts and ingredients to make this cake.

1. Take the same number of cups of brown sugar as the number of sons Zebedee had with him mending the nets.

2. The number of cups of milk are the number of camels Abraham's oldest servant took on his journey to find Rebekah as a wife for Isaac. Subtract the number of letters in the name of the apostle to whom it was said: Behold an Israelite in whom there in no guile.

3. For the cups of flour, take the number of fishes and divide by the number of loaves of bread when Jesus fed the 5,000.

4. The number of eggs (well beaten) are the number of days Paul stayed with Publis at Melita.

5. The number of teaspoons of baking powder is by adding the number of years Joshua lived to the number of years from the time God promised an inheritance to Caleb until the time he received it. Subtract the number of fishes the disciples caught at the sea of Tiberias. Add to your total the number one.

6. Find out what Herod swore he would give the daughter of Herodias. Take two cups and fill each one with the given amount of the promise and you will have the proper amount of shortening and butter.

He could hardly make sense of any of it.

Did you lie about your age to me Pat?

Dickey poured two beers.

A girl never tells her real age.

That picture you sent musta been taken ten years ago. Don't shuck? Ma thinks you're sixty if you're a day.

Padric stabbed his knitting needle back into the ball of turquoise yarn in his lap. Large moths thrashed their wings against the lamp shade. The dog took up the entire floor space.

Maybe a couple of years. Not ten. Did you expect a twinky? Did you let the moths in? Did you know I was a pastry baker? Would you like it if your wife wore women's panties?

Ma slid the answers under the door::

1. *2 cups brown sugar*
   Matt. 4:21
2. *1 cup sweet milk*
   Gen. 24:10, John 1:47
3. *2 1/2 cups flour*
   Matt. 14:17, Matt. 14:21
4. *3 eggs*
   Acts 28:8
5. *3 teaspoons baking powder*
   Judges 2:8, Jos. 14:10, John 21:11
6. *1/8 cup butter, 1/2 cup lard*
   Mark 6:23.

Padric left his annotations on a piece of scrap paper stuck into the flour-dusted black Bible.

The cake he baked was like a rock.

He returned to New York by train, arrived at Penn Station.

He slept on various AA couches.

The pawnbroker gave him two hundred thirty dollars for Dickey's mother's broach and the pouch of confederate coins he'd stolen.

His trunk arrived back two months later. Every piece of clothes—his trousseau—had been sliced into strips with a sharp knife. His photo was crumpled into a clot.

They gave him a general to put him to sleep. Then he was drugged in order to immobilize him completely so he wouldn't move during surgery. Would his wrecked body get back into balance? He'd willed the right mixture of gases to circulate in his blood, and hoped to keep his heartbeat consistent.

It took an hour to remove the veins from his right leg. Then the team opened his chest. The doctor turned on the heart-lung machine and clamped the aorta, stopping the blood supply to the heart. They clamped for about fifteen minutes and unclamped for five minutes to let the heart drink, clamped again and unclamped. A solution of potassium was injected to cool the heart down and stop the metabolic rate. When he was opened up there was no doubt he needed a double bypass.

While under the anesthetic, Padric discovered he was living in a rock pool filled with soothing liquid in which he lay suspended, naked, just below the surface staring out with two enormous eyes at what appeared to be a large cave with walls that glowed with primal colors.

He thought he was walking on fiery red mosaics. He could feel the pain of the fire, but it didn't burn. He felt a tearing pain, as if his body was being ripped in two. He felt a hard, cold core of ice melt onto the operating table. He thought, I've known about that ice for a long, long time. It's like an icicle of fear proving that I'm unworthy of love and no matter how hard I try to love ... he lost the thread of the dream, smelled astringent.

After the operation he dreamed about baboons. He was the hunter and he was in the jungle hunting baboons of all sizes and ages.

He was one hundred eighty pounds with a thirty-six inch waist before the operation. Afterwards he was one hundred sixty-five pounds and had a thirty-two inch waist.

During the operation he'd needed fourteen pints of blood. His AA friends gave more than fourteen.

He strolled up and down the hospital corridor with his green writer/biographer friend, Alison. They watched two men smoking. One was the middle-aged victim of a tracheotomy who smoked a cigarette through a hole in his throat. The hole was covered with a piece of gauze that got lifted to accommodate the cigarette. The other smoker was recovering from throat cancer, had a metallic robot's voice coming out of a mechanical voice box attached to his throat. He smoked Kools. The writer smoked Kent. Padric smoked his writer friend's Kents.

Stretched out on Tracy's brown couch under his own afghan, Serenity curled across his feet.

Padric shouted, Get six or so medium-sized white potatoes. A can of condensed cheddar cheese soup. A little can of pimiento. An onion.

I have onions. Don't shout.

Milk?

I have milk.

Old bread to make bread crumbs?

I'll get packaged bread crumbs. You need bread crumbs for soup?

No, I'm baking Potatoes O'Brien like Mary did. Your mother made *Pomme de Terre Chatouillard*, mine made O'Brien. One hundred percent Irish, like her heart.

Padric's bridge didn't meet the gum, his chest hurt, his legs hurt, his feet were swollen into the mahogany loafers from sitting for three days at the front of the bus in order to see the scenery and be close to the driver. In case.

The bus passed the trading post at Red Lake, Arizona. Beside the highway, two gigantic rocks—Elephant Feet. He dozed.

The bus passed Hoskinini Mesa where Kit Carson once made his Navajo roundup. Padric took out his teeth, stored them in the mesh sack with a Butterfinger Bar that hung on the back of the seat in front of him. He needed another Percodan. Took two. Out the window, two squarish, imposing buttes, Merrick and Mitchell, the names of the prospectors made rich with their silver, who, the know-it-all across the aisle explained, became consumed by greed and returned for more silver never to be heard from again. The bus had no air conditioner and his window wouldn't open. He nodded off. He dreamed of a sign that advertised a circus. The gaudy drawing showed a lion holding the jaw of a man open with his paws.

Arizona had space, rocks could be orange or brown, tan, rust, green, acid. He choked up when he saw live deer eating pine needles from long ponderosa pines. The bus made a rest stop. He smoked a few forbidden cigarettes. An Indian ran the stand and sold blankets, pots, mint-green ocotillo cactus jelly. Also jewelry, pottery, authentic and made by Navajos, Zunis and Pueblo Indians. From the convenience shop he bought a pint of gin but didn't touch it, only stored it with his razor. In case.

He demonstrated that he was fluent in every stitch. Saddle stitch, decorative tack, arrowhead tack, crow's foot tack, that he could do monograms, could embroider, knew the blanket stitch, cross stitch, fly stitch, herringbone stitch, chain stitch, lazy daisy stitch, French knot, feather stitch.

What about Frou Frou? Miss Maxine asked.

He told the queen, I can do fringes and tassels and pompons and ruffles and trifles and trims, if that's what you mean.

Can you trim with lace?

Yes.

Gathered lace?

Yes.

I can't hear you, what did you say?

He raised his voice, his denture wasn't gripping.

Yes, either commercially pre-gathered or pleated.

Edging?

Yes. Yes.

Hooks and eyes?

Yes.

Snaps?

Yes.

Snap tape?

Yes.

Shank buttons?

Yes.

Feathers?

Yeah, sure.

Fur?

Yes.

Braid?

Yes.

Binding?

Yes.

Bands?

Yes.

Rickrack?

Yes.

Collars?

Yes.

Cuffs?

Sure.

Frogs and Chinese ball buttons?

Finally Padric hit a blank wall and his eyes iced over.

I know nothing about frogs and Chinese ball buttons, Madam.

Miss Maxine couldn't resist asking, Knife pleats?

He didn't reply. Miss Maxine crossed her arms over her chest, squeezed her hands under her arms.

He was hired to sew mail order, three foot Cuddle Cocks in three shades of satin—pink, black, and white. Fairy Fred, a fifty-plus queen from Nebraska, gave him bolts of duchess satin and slipper satin to sew with in the mobile home they shared. Their trailer had a woodstove and a space heater that smelled of woodsmoke.

Miss Maxine told him under what conditions he could stay: You can live at the commune, receive food and a small allowance. In return you sew Cuddle Cocks for the commune in the workshop all day, one half hour for lunch, two fifteen-minute tea breaks ... provide your own tea ... six days a week. As long as your production keeps up with our mail orders you can stay. The commune lives off the proceeds of those pillows. Clear?

As consumé.

He got friendly with La Rosa, the boy at the commune who boxed and shipped the Cuddle Cocks. La Rosa confided that the reason he was here was that he was a member of a secret sect.

Oh ...

... of Penitentes. If you felt like it, you could come with me on Easter ... I'm going to join my people.

What form of transportation?

Thumb. I've been working here at the commune until I have enough money. I do now. Would you hitch-hike with me on the last leg of my journey? Of course you'd have to come back by yourself.

Padric accepted the invitation. They left on Sunday morning but very quickly he was tired, he crouched down on the side of the road while La Rosa stood at the edge, thumb out. Every muscle in his body hurt. He had never worked such long hours. His hands felt as though they'd been pounded by a hammer.

Padric didn't care to join but agreed to help—when La Rosa asked—to whip him. The whip was made of spiny cactus that stuck in La Rosa's back. When thoroughly whipped, bloody and scratched, La Rosa was attached to a large cross that was stuck into a field where beans and other vegetables grew.

Padric left him there in the vegetable field with other bloody men on makeshift crosses and hitch-hiked back to the commune on his own.

He developed a small, envelope-shaped belly. Having no muscle tone, it sagged rather than protruded. He called it: My envelope flap.

He told Miss Maxine, I need to do push-ups, something rigorous to get rid of this ugly, excess abdomen.

Miss Maxine didn't agree.

You need it. You're converting nectar into fat like a monarch butterfly does when preparing to migrate one thousand eight hundred miles or further.

Like a cushion. A winter cushion?

You'll see, when you hit the road again, you'll only need water to rehydrate your body not food. So tank up now.

Go? Where?

Miss Maxine's lips pressed together.

Cunning was Miss Maxine's middle name. She was inexhaustible, could outsew Padric, produce twice the number of Cuddle Cocks that he could. He coiled like a snake when Miss Maxine suggested sex.

You can't mean it?

I do. You seem like you'd be as tasty as a geriatric Peter Pan.

He wore a white cowboy hat and drank a dram of champagne in one go. The first alcohol in eleven years. He chain smoked Virginia Slims.

He removed the cowboy hat, slipped the noose over his head, and returned the hat to his head.

1981. Padric played bingo on Wednesday and Saturday night at the Halfway House in San Diego. He lived on SSI, had thin lips, ate fried eggs. His hair was butch, close-cropped, grey mixed with brown, more like Fred McMurry, the actor, than Veronica Lake, the once-upon-a-time siren. He plucked his eyebrows into thin lines to enhance his bright hazel eyes. He was thin, but his bottom was round and soft, the little belly ever-ready, but not for a migration. He was lucky at bingo, loved bingo.

He roamed through Old Town, passed an adobe building with an etched date, 1825, and sat in the tree-filled plaza watching pretty California boys and girls. A plaque:

U.S. Flag First Raised here in 1846

A sign and an arrow pointed:

Bazaar del Mundo

Jacki O., the counselor at the Halfway House, took the residents by van to visit Del Coronado.

La Grande Dame, Dwight, a young resident from Las Vegas squealed when the hotel came into view.

Padric swooned too at the sight of Victorian grandeur, tall red cupolas, turrets, gingerbread trim. Of course, how could he forget. This was where Tony Curtis, Jack Lemmon, and ... who was it? ... of course, Marilyn Monroe, rollicked in *Some Like It Hot*. He was dying to announce the discovery to the group, but couldn't remember the name of the missing star. But then again, he decided against any mention of "Some Like It Hot" because he realized that he was the only one old enough to remember it. But, who was the other actor?

Once a week he wrapped a turquoise chiffon scarf around his neck and walked across the city to the—always frothy, always an icy blue—Pacific. Not interested in the sea, he skirted the harbors of bobbing boats to the same grocer—La Groceria des Madres—where he bought a lottery ticket and a pack of Virginia Slims. Even a small jackpot would finance a trip to Ireland. The cigarettes were rationed out to last the week since the halfway house took most of his SSI check.

Walking back to the Halfway House he bumped into Jacki O. on her way to work. She gave him such a violent hug that tears filled his eyes. Just then a name came to mind that made him toss his head like a stallion. Of course, Eli Wallach. But then he doubted himself. Had he been thinking of *Some Like It Hot*. Or? Or? *The Misfits*?

Dear Alison,

My counselor gave the following to me to think about. I have it taped to this typewriter:

A Summary of the World—If we could shrink the Earth's population to a village of precisely 100 people with all existing human ratios, it would look like this: There would be 57 Asians, 21 Europeans, 14 from the Western Hemisphere (North and South) and 8 Africans. 51 would be female; 49 would be male; 70 would be nonwhite; 30 white. 70 would be non-Christian; 30 Christian. 50% of the entire world's wealth would be in the hands of only 6 people and all 6 would be citizens of the United States. 80 would live in substandard housing. 70 would be unable to read. 50 would suffer from malnutrition. 1 would be near death, 1 would be near birth. Only 1 would have a college education. No one would own a typewriter.

Where would I fit in, since I now own a typewriter, thanks to Dwight, this sad sack here at the halfway house who (I dare say) has a not so little crush on me.

Dear Alison,

I'm sober 2 years and 1 month.

Ireland is MY place. Except on bingo nights (Saturday and Wednesday) and AA meeting nights (Monday, Sunday), I read everything I can lay my hands on about Ireland. Remember: My mother Mary came from there when she was a little girl. I have not much strength for physical work these day. Arthritis in my beautiful hands, alas. Findhorn isn't practical any longer... Instead, when I win the lottery, before I die, I want to go to County Meath in Ireland to visit the neolithic stone burial tomb into which the sun pours through on one day of the year, December 21, at exactly 8:58 in the morning, releasing the dead souls waiting all year in the pitch black burial chamber to the beam of light which will light their way to the next world.

I'm ready too. I'm willing. Any minute now, I'll be able.

You may remember that Mary gave birth to twins, that one died. Not me. I read an article about hormones in a health magazine. It seems that in an occasional family of mice the mother mouse might give extra doses of male or female hormones to baby mice in utero in order to help females to keep up with male or vice versa. Could it be, that that's what happened to me in there with my twin? Or was I homosexual because I was infected with the mumps when I was a little boy? Could it be, by the way, that Mary was a nymphomaniac, giving birth to 14 children? You must chew that over when you write my life story.

By parcel post I'm sending you an afghan throw which I made myself. Toss it across that ugly couch you have. It'll spruce things up.

Send blessings. I'll be back if they ever let me out. Or, if I live, which I doubt I will, as I'm more than ready to pack it in. I sense I'll be "released" soon with no "parole."

Until we meet again, then, on earth, or on another plane, don't forget your friend,

Padric
San Diego, 1982

The End

AUTHOR'S BIO

Internationally known best-selling author Alison Leslie Gold has published fiction including *Clairvoyant, The Imagined Life of Lucia Joyce*. Jay Parini said about it: "A vividly written book that plays daringly in the no-mans-land between biography and fiction." A reviewer in the New York Times summed up another novel *The Devil's Mistress: The Diary of Eva Braun, The Woman Who Lived and Died With Hitler* as follows: "It's hard to forget a novel that spreads across the imagination like a mysterious and evil stain." This book was nominated for the National Book Award. Her nonfiction writing on the Holocaust and World War II has received special recognition. Among those who have singled her out as a protector and chronicler of Holocaust experiences is Elie Wiesel, who said of her: "Let us give recognition to Alison Gold. Without her and her talent of persuasion, without her writer's talent, too, this poignant account, vibrating with humanity, would not have been written." Her works include *Anne Frank Remembered*, *The Story of the Woman Who Helped to Hide Anne Frank*, written with and about Miep Gies, who hid Anne Frank and rescued Anne's diary and *Memories of Anne Frank: Reflections of a Childhood Friend*, written for young people about Hannah "Lies" (pronounced "lease") Goslar, Anne Frank's best friend. Both books are international best sellers translated into more than twenty languages. Neither Miep nor Hannah had been willing to tell their entire stories until meeting Alison. Also for young people, *A Special Fate*, about Chiune Sugihara the little-known Japanese diplomat who saved 6,000 Jews and others during the war.

The nonfiction book *Fiet's Vase and Other Stories of Survival, Europe 1939-1945*, 25 interviews with survivors, is her farewell to that subject matter, and, *Love in the Second Act*, 25 true stories of those who have found love later in life, is the first book exploring less dispiriting themes. Most recently she was invited to write a short work for the Cahier Series (Am. Univ. Paris/Sylph Editions) titled *Lost and Found* soon followed by the publication of a literary novel *The Woman Who Brought Matisse Back from the Dead*, and a family story of alcoholic intervention for ages 10-13 co-authored with Darin Elliott—*Elephant in the Living Room*. Her nonfiction work has received awards ranging from the Best of the Best Award given by the American Library

Association, to a Merit of Educational Distinction Award by the Anti-Defamation League, and a Christopher Award affirming the highest values of the human spirit, among others. She divides her time between New York and an island in Greece. Four of her indelible works have been reissued with new material by innovative TMI Publishing, Providence, RI.

Printed in Great
Britain
by Amazon